THE CLASSIC POEMS

POEMS

ROBERT BURNS

EDITED BY
GEORGE DAVIDSON

CHARTWELL
BOOKS, INC.

This edition printed in 2010 by
CHARTWELL BOOKS, INC.
A Division of **BOOK SALES, INC.**
276 Fifth Avenue Suite 206
New York, New York 10001 USA

ISBN-13: 978-0-7858-2614-9
ISBN-10: 0-7858-2614-9
AD001389EN

3/11
B9 T
8.99

821.6
BURNS

Printed in China

Contents

HIGHLAND FLING.

INTRODUCTION

Some rhyme a neebor's name to lash;
Some rhyme (vain thought!) for needfu' cash;
Some rhyme to court the countra clash,
        An' raise a din;
For me, an aim I never fash;
        I rhyme for fun.[1]

I rhyme for fun. In these words in his *Epistle to James Smith*, written during the winter of 1785-86 when he would therefore be about twenty-seven, Burns summed up what made him a poet: he wrote poetry not for money, not for fame, not to mock or castigate, but basically for his own enjoyment. But to say with Burns that he wrote 'for fun' is certainly not to say that his poetic output, either before or after that time, consists solely of light-hearted and amusing songs and verses, though he did of course write many of these. As even this short collection of his best-known work clearly demonstrates, Burns was a master of many styles of poetry and song, from love songs and drinking songs to humorous verse, narrative poetry and biting satire, and even to prayers and psalms (these a part of Burns' poetic output less well known than they deserve to be). And as this collection equally shows, while Burns wrote for the most part in his own Scots dialect, he was just as capable of producing great poetry in perfect English, and indeed may skilfully and successfully make use of the two dialects in a single poem.

There can be few people who have heard of Robert Burns who do not know the date of his birth, or at least the day and the month: Burns Suppers are held the world over on or around his birthday, 25 January. Burns was born at Alloway,

at that time near (but now part of) the town of Ayr on the west coast of Scotland, in 1759. His father, William Burnes, was a tenant farmer, and it was while working on his father's farm in the autumn of 1774, that Burns, at the age of fifteen, 'first committed the sin of Rhyme', as he himself put it, in a love poem dedicated to the 14-year-old Nelly Kilpatrick (or Kirkpatrick) who was working alongside him at the harvest.

Burns and his brother Gilbert had three years of formal education between 1765 and 1768, but after the schoolmaster moved away their education was for a time continued by William Burnes himself. In 1773 Robert had a few further weeks of study under his former teacher, during which time he was introduced to the poetry of Alexander Pope. He was a voracious reader, at mealtimes eating with a spoon in one hand and a book in the other, and always carrying books with him to the fields in order to read in spare moments.

His father having moved to a farm at nearby Tarbolton, in 1780 Burns and a few friends formed the Tarbolton Bachelors' Club as a 'diversion to relieve the wearied man worn down with the necessary labours of life'. However, in 1781 Burns moved to Irvine to become a flax-dresser, a job which ended less than a year later when the premises burned down, leaving Burns in his own words 'a true poet, not worth a sixpence'. He returned to Tarbolton, but after the death of his father in 1784, the family moved to another farm, Mossgiel, near Mauchline.

In 1785, Burns became a father for the first time when his mother's servant-girl, Betty Paton, bore him a daughter. That same year he also met Jean Armour, with whom he went through what he referred to as 'some sort

of Wedlock', but he was rejected as a son-in-law by Jean's father. Jean having in September 1786 borne him twins, the 'feelings of a father' persuaded Burns to abandon plans he had to emigrate to the West Indies.

While he may not have intended to write poetry for 'needfu' cash', Burns had by this time decided to have his work published. The first edition of his poems, the Kilmarnock Edition, was published in 1786, after which Burns travelled to Edinburgh to try to have a second edition published there. The first Edinburgh Edition was published in 1787, followed by a second Edinburgh Edition in 1793.

In the spring of 1788, Jean bore another set of twins, who sadly died soon after. In June Burns left Ayrshire and established himself as a farmer at Ellisland, near Dumfries in the south of Scotland; Jean joined him there in the following December. In the same year, Burns was also trained and commissioned as an excise officer. By 1790, he was having to ride up to 200 miles a week on his excise duties while at the same time attempting to run a farm. This was having a serious effect on his health, and in 1791 Burns gave up the farm and the family moved to Dumfries, where in 1792 he was appointed to the Dumfries Port excise division. He must have been efficient at his job as at the end of 1794 he was appointed Acting Supervisor of Excise for Dumfries.

However, a year later, Burns was severely ill with rheumatic fever. His poor condition cannot have been helped by the famine that occurred in Dumfries at the beginning of 1796, when as Burns says, his family, like hundreds of others, were 'absolutely without one grain of meal'. He died in Dumfries on 21 July 1796, at the untimely age of 37. His last child, his son Maxwell, was born four days later, on the day of the funeral.

In his *Epistle to James Smith*, Burns had expressed fears that he would not be remembered as a poet:

There's ither poets, much your betters,
Far seen in Greek, deep men o' letters,
Hae thought they had ensur'd their debtors,
            A' future ages;
Now moths deform, in shapeless tatters,
            Their unknown pages.

Then farewell hopes o' Laurel-boughs
To garland my poetic brows!
Henceforth I'll rove where busy ploughs
            Are whistling thrang;
An' teach the lanely heights an' howes
            My rustic sang.

I'll wander on, wi' tentless heed
How never-halting moments speed,
Till Fate shall snap the brittle thread;
            Then, all unknown,
I'll lay me with th' inglorious dead,
            Forgot and gone![2]

We know now, as he could not have known or even guessed then, that his fame as Scotland's greatest poet has never died. He is certainly not forgotten, nor will he ever be.

George Davidson

[1] **countra clash** – country gossip; **din** – fuss, talk; **fash** – think about

[2] **ither** – other; **far seen** – well versed; **hae** – have; **a'** – all; **thrang** – busily; **lanely** – lonely; **howes** – valleys; **wi' tentless heed** – heedlessly; **forgot** – forgotten

To a Mountain Daisy,
On turning one down with the Plough

Wee, modest, crimson-tipped flow'r,
Thou's met me in an evil hour;
For I maun crush amang the stoure
        Thy slender stem:
To spare thee now is past my pow'r,
        Thou bonie gem.

Alas! it's no thy neebor sweet,
The bonie lark, companion meet,
Bending thee 'mang the dewy weet,
        Wi' spreckl'd breast,
When upward-springing, blythe, to greet
        The purpling East.

Cauld blew the bitter-biting North
Upon thy early, humble birth;
Yet cheerfully thou glinted forth
        Amid the storm,
Scarce rear'd above the Parent-earth
        Thy tender form.

The flaunting flow'rs our Gardens yield,
High shelt'ring woods and wa's maun shield;
But thou, beneath the random bield
        O' clod or stane,

Adorns the histie stibble-field,
            Unseen, alane.

There, in thy scanty mantle clad,
Thy snawie bosom sun-ward spread,
Thou lifts thy unassuming head
            In humble guise;
But now the share uptears thy bed,
            And low thou lies!

Such is the fate of artless Maid,
Sweet flow'ret of the rural shade!
By love's simplicity betray'd,
            And guileless trust;
Till she, like thee, all soil'd, is laid
            Low i' the dust.

Such is the fate of simple Bard,
On life's rough ocean luckless starr'd!
Unskilful he to note the card
            Of prudent lore,
Till billows rage, and gales blow hard,
            And whelm him o'er!

Such fate to suffering Worth is giv'n,
Who long with wants and woes has striv'n,
By human pride or cunning driv'n
            To Mis'ry's brink;

Till, wrench'd of ev'ry stay but Heav'n,
      He, ruin'd, sink!

Ev'n thou who mourn'st the Daisy's fate,
That fate is thine – no distant date;
Stern Ruin's plough-share drives elate,
      Full on thy bloom,
Till crush'd beneath the furrow's weight,
      Shall be thy doom!

TERMS maun – must; **amang** – among; **stoure** – dust; **bonie** – pretty;
no – not; **neebor** – neighbour; **'mang** – among; **weet** – wet; **spreckl'd**
– speckled; **blythe** – cheerful; **cauld** – cold; **wa's** – walls; **bield** – shelter;
stane – stone; **histie** – bare, barren; **stibble** – stubble; **alane** – alone;
snawie – snowy; **card** – chart

• *The verse-form used in this poem is known as the 'Burns stanza'. Although
he did not originate this verse structure, Burns makes frequent use of it, and it is
especially associated with his poetry.*

To a Mouse,
On turning her up in her Nest with the Plough

Wee, sleekit, cow'rin, tim'rous beastie,
O, what a panic's in thy breastie!
Thou need na start awa sae hasty,
     Wi' bickering brattle!
I wad be laith to rin an' chase thee,
     Wi' murdering pattle!

I'm truly sorry Man's dominion
Has broken Nature's social union,
An' justifies that ill opinion,
     Which makes thee startle
At me, thy poor, earth-born companion,
     An' fellow-mortal!

I doubt na, whyles, but thou may thieve;
What then? poor beastie, thou maun live!
A daimen icker in a thrave
     'S a sma' request;
I'll get a blessin wi' the lave,
     An' never miss 't!

Thy wee-bit housie, too, in ruin!
It's silly wa's the win's are strewin'!
An' naething, now, to big a new ane,

O' foggage green!
An' bleak December's win's ensuin,
Baith snell an' keen!

Thou saw the fields laid bare an' waste,
An' weary winter comin fast,
An' cozie here, beneath the blast,
Thou thought to dwell,
Till crash! the cruel coulter past
Out thro' thy cell.

That wee-bit heap o' leaves an' stibble,
Has cost thee monie a weary nibble!
Now thou's turn'd out, for a' thy trouble,
But house or hald,
To thole the winter's sleety dribble,
An' cranreuch cauld!

But Mousie, thou art no thy lane,
In proving foresight may be vain:
The best-laid schemes o' Mice an' Men
Gang aft agley,
An' lea'e us nought but grief an' pain,
For promis'd joy!

Still thou art blest, compar'd wi' me
The present only toucheth thee:
But, Och! I backward cast my e'e,

On prospects drear!
An' forward, tho' I canna see,
I guess an' fear!

TERMS sleekit – sleek; **breastie** – breast; **na** – not; **awa** – away; **sae** – so; **wi' bickering brattle** – in a scurry; **wad** – would; **laith** – loath; **rin** – run; **pattle** – plough-scraper; **whyles** – sometimes; **maun** – must; **a daimen icker in a thrave** – an occasional ear of corn in 24 sheaves; **sma'** – small; **the lave** – what is left; **wee-bit** – small; **silly wa's** – feeble walls; **win's** – winds; **big** – build; **ane** – one; **foggage** – coarse grass; **baith** – both; **snell** – sharp, bitter; **coulter** – ploughshare; **past** – passed; **stibble** – stubble; **monie** – many; **a'** – all; **but house or hald** – without house or home; **thole** – endure; **cranreuch cauld** – cold hoar frost; **no thy lane** – not alone; **gang aft agley** – often go awry; **lea'e** – leave; **e'e** – eye; **canna** – cannot

The Cotter's Saturday Night

Let not Ambition mock their useful toil,
Their homely joys, and destiny obscure;
Nor Grandeur hear, with a disdainful smile,
The short and simple annals of the Poor. – Gray

My lov'd, my honor'd, much respected friend!

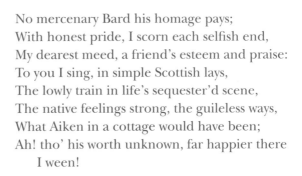

No mercenary Bard his homage pays;
With honest pride, I scorn each selfish end,
My dearest meed, a friend's esteem and praise:
To you I sing, in simple Scottish lays,
The lowly train in life's sequester'd scene,
The native feelings strong, the guileless ways,
What Aiken in a cottage would have been;
Ah! tho' his worth unknown, far happier there
    I ween!

November chill blaws loud wi' angry sugh;
The short'ning winter-day is near a close;
The miry beasts retreating frae the pleugh;
The black'ning trains o' craws to their repose:
The toil-worn Cotter frae his labour goes,
This night his weekly moil is at an end,
Collects his spades, his mattocks, and his hoes,
Hoping the morn in ease and rest to spend,
And weary, o'er the moor, his course does
    hameward bend.

At length his lonely Cot appears in view,
Beneath the shelter of an aged tree;
Th' expectant wee-things, toddlan, stacher
    through
To meet their Dad, wi' flichterin noise and glee.
His wee-bit ingle, blinkan bonilie,
His clean hearth-stane, his thrifty Wifie's smile,

The lisping infant, prattling on his knee,
Does a' his weary kiaugh and care beguile,
An' makes him quite forget his labor and
    his toil.

Belyve, the elder bairns come drapping in,
At Service out, amang the Farmers roun';
Some ca' the pleugh, some herd, some
    tentie rin
A cannie errand to a neebor town:
Their eldest hope, their Jenny, woman-
    grown,
In youthfu' bloom, Love sparkling in her e'e,
Comes hame, perhaps to show a braw new
    gown,
Or deposite her sair-won penny-fee,
To help her Parents dear, if they in hardship
    be.

With joy unfeign'd, brothers and sisters
    meet,
And each for other's weelfare kindly speirs:
The social hours, swift-wing'd, unnotic'd,
    fleet;
Each tells the uncos that he sees or hears.
The Parents partial eye their hopeful years;
Anticipation forward points the view;
The Mother, wi' her needle and her sheers,

Gars auld claes look amaist as weel's the new;
The Father mixes a' wi' admonition due.

Their Master's and their Mistress's command,
The younkers a' are warned to obey;
And mind their labors wi' an eydent hand,
And ne'er, tho' out o' sight, to jauk or play:
'And O! be sure to fear the Lord alway!
And mind your duty, duly, morn and night!
Lest in temptation's path ye gang astray,
Implore His counsel and assisting might:
They never sought in vain that sought the Lord
    aright.'

But hark! a rap comes gently to the door;
Jenny, wha kens the meaning o' the same,
Tells how a neebor lad came o'er the moor,
To do some errands, and convoy her hame.
The wily Mother sees the conscious flame
Sparkle in Jenny's e'e, and flush her cheek;
With heart-struck anxious care, enquires
    his name,
While Jenny hafflins is afraid to speak;
Weel-pleased the Mother hears, it's nae wild,
    worthless Rake.

With kindly welcome, Jenny brings him ben;
A strappan youth, he takes the Mother's eye;

Blythe Jenny sees the visit's no ill ta'en;
The Father cracks of horses, pleughs, and kye.
The youngster's artless heart o'erflows wi' joy,
But blate an' laithfu', scarce can weel behave;
The Mother, wi' a woman's wiles, can spy
What makes the youth sae bashfu' and
    sae grave,
Weel-pleas'd to think her bairn's respected
    like the lave.

O happy love! where love like this is found:
O heart-felt raptures! bliss beyond compare!
I've paced much this weary, mortal round,
And sage Experience bids me this declare –
'If Heaven a draught of heavenly pleasure
    spare,
One cordial in this melancholy vale,
'Tis when a youthful, loving, modest Pair
In other's arms, breathe out the tender tale,
Beneath the milk-white thorn that scents the
    ev'ning gale.'

Is there, in human form, that bears a heart –
A wretch! a villain! lost to love and truth!
That can, with studied, sly, ensnaring art,
Betray sweet Jenny's unsuspecting youth?
Curse on his perjur'd arts! dissembling,
    smoothe!

Are Honor, Virtue, Conscience, all exil'd?
Is there no Pity, no relenting Ruth,
Points to the parents fondling o'er their Child?
Then paints the ruin'd Maid, and their
    distraction wild?

But now the Supper crowns their simple board,
The halesome Porritch, chief o' Scotia's food;
The soupe their only Hawkie does afford,
That 'yont the hallan snugly chows her cood:
The Dame brings forth, in complimental mood,
To grace the lad, her weel-hain'd kebbuck, fell;
And aft he's prest, and aft he ca's it guid;
The frugal Wifie, garrulous, will tell,
How 'twas a towmond auld, sin Lint was i'
    the bell.

The chearfu' Supper done, wi' serious face,
They, round the ingle, form a circle wide;
The Sire turns o'er, with patriarchal grace,
The big ha'-Bible, ance his Father's pride:
His bonnet rev'rently is laid aside,
His lyart haffets wearing thin and bare;
Those strains that once did sweet in Zion glide,
He wales a portion with judicious care;
'And let us worship God!' he says, with
    solemn air.

They chant their artless notes in simple guise,
They tune their hearts, by far the noblest aim;
Perhaps *Dundee's* wild-warbling measures rise,
Or plaintive *Martyrs*, worthy of the name;
Or noble *Elgin* beets the heaven-ward flame;
The sweetest far of Scotia's holy lays:
Compar'd with these, Italian trills are tame;
The tickl'd ears no heart-felt raptures raise;
Nae unison hae they, with our Creator's praise.

The priest-like Father reads the sacred page,
How Abram was the Friend of God on high;
Or, Moses bade eternal warfare wage
With Amalek's ungracious progeny;
Or, how the royal Bard did groaning lye
Beneath the stroke of Heaven's avenging ire;
Or Job's pathetic plaint, and wailing cry;
Or rapt Isaiah's wild, seraphic fire;
Or other Holy Seers that tune the sacred lyre.

Perhaps the Christian Volume is the theme:
How guiltless blood for guilty man was shed;
How He, who bore in Heaven the second
    name,
Had not on Earth whereon to lay His head:
How His first followers and servants sped;
The Precepts sage they wrote to many a land:
How he, who lone in Patmos banished,

23

Saw in the sun a mighty angel stand,
And heard great Bab'lon's doom pronounc'd by
    Heaven's command.

Then kneeling down to Heaven's Eternal King,
The Saint, the Father, and the Husband prays:
Hope 'springs exulting on triumphant wing',
That thus they all shall meet in future days,
There, ever bask in uncreated rays,
No more to sigh, or shed the bitter tear,
Together hymning their Creator's praise,
In such society, yet still more dear;
While circling Time moves round in an eternal
    sphere

Compar'd with this, how poor Religion's pride,
In all the pomp of method, and of art;
When men display to congregations wide
Devotion's ev'ry grace, except the heart!
The Power, incens'd, the Pageant will desert,
The pompous strain, the sacerdotal stole;
But haply, in some Cottage far apart,
May hear, well-pleas'd, the language of the Soul;
And in His Book of Life the Inmates poor enroll.

Then homeward all take off their sev'ral way;
The youngling Cottagers retire to rest:
The Parent-pair their secret homage pay,

And proffer up to Heaven the warm request,
That 'He who stills the raven's clam'rous nest,
And decks the lily fair in flow'ry pride,
Would, in the way His Wisdom sees the best,
For them and for their little ones provide;
But chiefly, in their hearts with Grace Divine
    preside'.

From Scenes like these, old Scotia's grandeur
    springs,
That makes her lov'd at home, rever'd abroad:
Princes and lords are but the breath of kings,
'An honest man's the noble work of God';
And certes, in fair Virtue's heavenly road,
The Cottage leaves the Palace far behind;
What is a lordling's pomp? a cumbrous load,
Disguising oft the wretch of human kind,
Studied in arts of Hell, in wickedness refin'd!

O Scotia! my dear, my native soil!
For whom my warmest wish to Heaven is sent!
Long may thy hardy sons of rustic toil
Be blest with health, and peace, and sweet
    content!
And O! may Heaven their simple lives prevent
From Luxury's contagion, weak and vile!
Then, howe'er crowns and coronets be rent,
A virtuous Populace may rise the while,

And stand a wall of fire around their much-
   lov'd Isle.

O Thou! who pour'd the patriotic tide,
That stream'd thro' Wallace's undaunted
   heart,
Who dar'd to, nobly, stem tyrannic pride,
Or nobly die, the second glorious part:
(The patriot's God, peculiarly Thou art,
His friend, inspirer, guardian, and reward!)
O never, never Scotia's realm desert;
But still the Patriot, and the Patriot-bard
In bright succession raise, her Ornament
   and Guard!

TERMS cotter – tenant or farmworker occupying a cottage with his family;
blaws – blows; **sugh** – the wailing or roaring sound of the wind; **frae the
pleugh** – from the plough; **craws** – crows; **hameward** – homeward;
cot – cottage; **wee-things** – small children; **toddlan** – toddling; **stacher**
– stagger, totter; **flichterin** – running with open arms to greet someone;
wee-bit ingle – small fire; **blinkan bonilie** – burning nicely; **kiaugh** –
anxiety, worry; **belyve** – soon; **bairns** – children; **amang** – among; **ca'
the pleugh** – drive the plough; **tentie** – with care; **rin a cannie errand**
– run a careful errand; **neebor** – neighbouring; **e'e** – eye; **hame** – home;
braw – lovely; **sair-won penny-fee** – hard-earned wages; **speirs**
– asks; **uncos** – news, gossip; **sheers** – scissors; **gars** – makes; **claes**
– clothes; **amaist** – almost; **younkers** – youngsters; **eydent** – diligent,
conscientious; **jauk** – fool about; **gang** – go

wha kens – who knows; **neebor** – neighbour; **hafflins** – almost; **nae** – no; **ben** – inside; **strappan** – strapping; **ta'en** – taken; **cracks** – talks, chats; **pleughs** – ploughs; **kye** – cattle; **blate an' laithfu'** – shy and bashful; **the lave** – the rest; **other's** – each other's; **thorn** – hawthorn; **halesome porritch** – wholesome porridge; **soupe** – drink; **Hawkie** – name given to a cow; **'yont the hallan** – beyond the partition; **chows her cood** – chews the cud; **weel-hain'd kebbuck** – well-matured cheese; **fell** – strong, tasty; **aft** – often; **ca's** – calls; **guid** – good; **towmond** – year; **sin Lint was i' the bell** – since flax was in flower; **ingle** – fire; **ha'-Bible** – large family Bible; **ance** – once; **lyart haffets** – grey-streaked sidelocks; **wales** – chooses; **beets** – adds fuel to, fans; **nae** – no; **hae** – have; **youngling** – young, youthful

Address to a Haggis

Fair fa' your honest, sonsie face,
Great Chieftain o' the Puddin'-race!
Aboon them a' ye tak your place,
    Painch, tripe, or thairm:
Weel are ye wordy of a grace
    As lang's my arm.

The groaning trencher there ye fill,
Your hurdies like a distant hill,
Your pin wad help to mend a mill
    In time o' need,

While thro' your pores the dews distil
     Like amber bead.

His knife see Rustic-labour dight,
An' cut you up wi' ready slight,
Trenching your gushing entrails bright,
     Like onie ditch;
And then, O what a glorious sight,
     Warm-reekin, rich!

Then, horn for horn, they stretch an' strive:
Deil tak the hindmost, on they drive,
Till a' their weel-swall'd kytes belyve
     Are bent like drums;
Then auld Guidman, maist like to rive,
     Bethankit hums.

Is there that owre his French ragout
Or olio that wad staw a sow,
Or fricassee wad make her spew
     Wi' perfect sconner,
Looks down wi' sneering, scornfu' view
     On sic a dinner?

Poor devil! see him owre his trash,
As feckless as a wither'd rash,
His spindle shank a guid whip-lash,
     His nieve a nit;

Thro' bluidy flood or field to dash,
        O how unfit!

But mark the Rustic, haggis-fed,
The trembling earth resounds his tread,
Clap in his walie nieve a blade,
        He'll mak it whissle;
An' legs, an' arms, an' heads will sned,
        Like taps o' thrissle.

Ye Pow'rs, wha mak mankind your care,
And dish them out their bill o' fare,
Auld Scotland wants nae skinking ware
        That jaups in luggies;
But, if ye wish her gratefu' prayer,
        Gie her a Haggis!

TERMS fair fa' – good luck to; **sonsie** – cheerful; **puddin'** – sausage;
aboon – above; **painch** – paunch, stomach; **thairm** – intestines; **wordy**
– worthy; **hurdies** – haunches; **pin** – skewer; **dight** – wipe; **slight** – skill;
onie – any; **reekin** – steaming; **horn** – horn spoon; **weel-swall'd kytes**
– well-swollen bellies; **belyve** – soon; **auld Guidman** – old Goodman, the
head of the household; **maist like to rive** – almost bursting; **Bethankit**
– 'God be thanked'; **owre** – over; **staw** – sicken; **sconner** – disgust; **sic** –
such; **rash** – rush; **spindle shank** – thin leg; **nieve** – fist; **nit** – nut; **bluidy**
– bloody; **clap in his walie nieve** – put in his strong fist; **sned** – cut off;
taps o' thrissle – heads of thistles; **wha mak** – who make; **skinking** –
watery; **jaups in luggies** – splashes about in bowls

To a Louse,
On Seeing One on a Lady's Bonnet
at Church

Ha! whare ye gaun, ye crowlan ferlie!
Your impudence protects you sairly:
I canna say but ye strunt rarely
  Owre gauze and lace;
Tho' faith, I fear ye dine but sparely
  On sic a place.

Ye ugly, creepan, blastet wonner,
Detested, shunn'd by saunt an' sinner,
How daur ye set your fit upon her –
  Sae fine a Lady!
Gae somewhere else and seek your dinner
  On some poor body.

Swith, in some beggar's haffet squattle;
There ye may creep, and sprawl, and sprattle,
Wi' ither kindred, jumping cattle,
  In shoals and nations;
Whare horn nor bane ne'er daur unsettle
  Your thick plantations.

Now haud you there, ye're out o' sight,
Below the fatt'rels, snug and tight;
Na, faith ye yet! ye'll no be right,

Till ye've got on it,
The vera tapmost, tow'ring height
O' Miss's bonnet.

My sooth! right bauld ye set your nose out,
As plump an' grey as onie grozet:
O for some rank, mercurial rozet,
Or fell, red smeddum,
I'd gie you sic a hearty dose o't,
Wad dress your droddum.

I wad na been surpris'd to spy
You on an auld wife's flainen toy;
Or aiblins some bit duddie boy,
On 's wylecoat;
But Miss's fine Lunardi, fye!
How daur ye do't?

O Jenny, dinna toss your head,
An' set your beauties a' abread!
Ye little ken what cursed speed
The blastie's makin:
Thae winks an' finger-ends, I dread,
Are notice takin.

O wad some Pow'r the giftie gie us
To see oursels as ithers see us!
It wad frae monie a blunder free us,

An' foolish notion:
What airs in dress an' gait wad lea'e us,
An' ev'n Devotion!

TERMS whare ye gaun? – where are you going?; **crowlan ferlie** – crawling oddity; **sairly** – well; **canna** – cannot; **strunt rarely** – strut well; **owre** – over; **sic** – such; **creepan** – creeping; **blastet wonner** – blasted wonder; **saunt** – saint; **daur** – dare; **fit** – foot; **gae** – go; **swith** – away with you!; **haffet squattle** – squat temples; **sprattle** – scramble; **ither** – other; **cattle** – beasts, insects, lice; **horn nor bane** – horn or bone combs; **haud you there** – just stay there; **fatt'rels** – ribbons, trimmings; **faith ye yet** – confound you; **vera tapmost** – very topmost; **bauld** – bold; **onie grozet** – any gooseberry; **rozet** – resin; **fell red smeddum** – poisonous red powder; **wad dress your droddum** – would give you what for; **wad na been** – would not have been; **flainen toy** – flannel cap; **aiblins** – perhaps; **duddie** – ragged; **wylecoat** – undervest; **Lunardi** – bonnet; **dinna** – don't; **a' abread** – all abroad; **blastie** – pest; **thae** – those; **finger-ends** – pointing fingers; **giftie** – ability; **monie** – many; **lea'e** – leave

On Seeing a Wounded Hare Limp by Me, which a Fellow had Just Shot

Inhuman man! curse on thy barb'rous art,
And blasted be thy murder-aiming eye!
May never pity soothe thee with a sigh,
Nor ever pleasure glad thy cruel heart!

Go live, poor wanderer of the wood and field!
The bitter little that of life remains:
No more the thickening brakes and verdant
    plains
To thee shall home, or food, or pastime yield.

Seek, mangled wretch, some place of wonted
    rest,
No more of rest, but now thy dying bed!
The sheltering rushes whistling o'er thy head,
The cold earth with thy bloody bosom prest.

Oft as by winding Nith I, musing, wait
The sober eve, or hail the cheerful dawn,
I'll miss thee sporting o'er the dewy lawn,
And curse the ruffian's aim, and mourn thy
    hapless fate.

 ## Address to the Tooth-ache

My curse on your envenom'd stang,
That shoots my tortur'd gums alang,
An' thro' my lugs gies mony a bang,
      Wi' gnawin vengeance,
Tearing my nerves wi' bitter twang,
      Like racking engines!

A' down my beard the slavers trickle,
I cast the wee stools o'er the meikle,
While round the fire the hav'rels keckle,
      To see me loup;
I curse an' ban, an' wish a heckle
      Were i' their doup!

Whan fevers burn, or agues freeze us,
Rheumatics gnaw, or colics squeeze us,
Our neebors sympathise, to ease us,
      Wi' pitying moan;
But thee – thou hell o' a' diseases,
      They mock our groan.

O' a' the num'rous human dools,
Ill-hairsts, daft bargains, cutty-stools,
Or worthy frien's laid i' the mools,
      Sad sight to see!

The tricks o' knaves, or fash o' fools,
　　　Thou bear'st the gree.

Whare'er that place be, priests ca' hell,
Whare a' the tones o' misery yell,
An' plagues in ranked number tell,
　　　In dreadfu' raw,
Thou, Tooth-ache, surely bear'st the bell,
　　　Aboon them a'!

O! thou grim, mischief-making chiel,
That gars the notes o' discord squeel,
Till human-kind aft dance a reel
　　　In gore a shoe-thick,
Gie a' the faes o' Scotland's weal
　　　A towmond's tooth-ache!

TERMS stang – stinging pain; **alang** – along; **lugs** – ears; **gies mony a bang** – gives many a pain; **twang** – twinge; **a'** – all; **meikle** – large; **hav'rels keckle** – fools cackle; **loup** – hop around; **heckle** – flax-comb; **doup** – buttocks; **neebors** – neighbours; **a'** – all; **dools** – woes; **ill-hairsts** – bad harvests; **cutty-stool** – the seat in a church where a person guilty of some misconduct had to sit in shame on a Sunday; **frien's** – friends; **mools** – earth (of a grave); **fash** – annoyance; **bear'st the gree** – take the prize; **whare'er** – wherever; **ca'** – call; **raw** – row; **aboon** – above; **chiel** – fellow; **gars** – makes; **aft** – often; **gie** – give; **faes** – foes; **weal** – welfare; **towmond** – twelve-month, year

 ## Address to the Deil

O Prince! O Chief of many throned pow'rs!
That led th' embattl'd seraphim to war – Milton

O Thou! whatever title suit thee –
Auld Hornie, Satan, Nick, or Clootie –
Wha in yon cavern grim an' sootie,
    Clos'd under hatches,
Spairges about the brunstane cootie,
    To scaud poor wretches!

Hear me, auld Hangie, for a wee,
An' let poor damned bodies be;
I'm sure sma' pleasure it can gie,
    Ev'n to a deil,
To skelp an' scaud poor dogs like me,
    An' hear us squeel!

Great is thy pow'r an' great thy fame;
Far kend an' noted is thy name;
An' tho' yon lowan heugh's thy hame,
    Thou travels far;
An' faith! thou's neither lag, nor lame,
    Nor blate, nor scaur.

Whyles, ranging like a roarin lion,
For prey, a' holes and corners tryin;

Whyles, on the strong-wind'd Tempest flyin,
    Tirlan the kirks;
Whyles, in the human bosom pryin,
    Unseen thou lurks.

I've heard my rev'rend Graunie say,
In lanely glens ye like to stray;
Or where auld ruin'd castles grey
    Nod to the moon,
Ye fright the nightly wand'rer's way,
    Wi' eldritch croon.

When twilight did my Graunie summon,
To say her pray'rs, douce, honest woman!
Aft yont the dyke she's heard you bumman,
    Wi' eerie drone;
Or, rustlin, thro' the boortries coman,
    Wi' heavy groan.

Ae dreary, windy, winter night,
The stars shot down wi' sklentan light,
Wi' you, myself, I gat a fright,
    Ayont the lough;
Ye, like a rash-buss, stood in sight,
    Wi' waving sugh.

The cudgel in my nieve did shake,
Each brist'ld hair stood like a stake,

When wi' an eldritch, stoor *quaick, quaick*,
    Amang the springs,
Awa ye squatter'd like a drake,
    On whistling wings.

Let Warlocks grim, an' wither'd Hags,
Tell how wi' you, on ragweed nags,
They skim the muirs an' dizzy crags,
    Wi' wicked speed;
And in kirk-yards renew their leagues,
    Owre howket dead.

Thence, countra wives, wi' toil and pain,
May plunge an' plunge the kirn in vain;
For Och! the yellow treasure's ta'en
    By witching skill;
An' dawtit, twal-pint Hawkie's gane
    As yell 's the Bill.

Thence, mystic knots mak great abuse
On Young-Guidmen, fond, keen an' croose,
When the best warklum i' the house,
    By cantraip wit,
Is instant made no worth a louse,
    Just at the bit.

When thowes dissolve the snawy hoord,
An' float the jinglin icy boord,

Then Water-kelpies haunt the foord,
    By your direction,
An' nighted Trav'llers are allur'd
    To their destruction.

And aft your moss-traversing Spunkies
Decoy the wight that late an' drunk is:
The bleezan, curst, mischievous monkies
    Delude his eyes,
Till in some miry slough he sunk is,
    Ne'er mair to rise.

When Masons' mystic word an' grip
In storms an' tempests raise you up,
Some cock or cat your rage maun stop,
    Or, strange to tell!
The youngest Brother ye wad whip
    Aff straught to Hell.

Lang syne in Eden's bonie yard,
When youthfu' lovers first were pair'd,
An' all the Soul of Love they shar'd,
    The raptur'd hour,
Sweet on the fragrant flow'ry swaird,
    In shady bow'r:

Then you, ye auld, snick-drawing dog!
Ye cam to Paradise incog,

An' play'd on man a cursed brogue,
   (Black be your fa'!)
An' gied the infant warld a shog,
   'Maist ruin'd a'.

D'ye mind that day when in a bizz
Wi' reeket duds, an' reestet gizz,
Ye did present your smoutie phiz
   'Mang better folk,
An' sklented on the man of Uzz
   Your spitefu' joke?

An' how ye gat him i' your thrall,
An' brak him out o' house an hal',
While scabs and botches did him gall,
   Wi' bitter claw;
An' lows'd his ill-tongu'd wicked Scawl –
   Was warst ava?

But a' your doings to rehearse,
Your wily snares an' fechtin fierce,
Sin' that day Michael did you pierce,
   Down to this time,
Wad ding a Lallan tounge, or Erse,
   In Prose or Rhyme.

An' now, auld Cloots, I ken ye're thinkan,
A certain bardie's rantin, drinkin,

Some luckless hour will send him linkan
    To your black pit;
But faith! he'll turn a corner jinkan,
    An' cheat you yet.

But fare-you-weel, auld Nickie-ben!
O wad ye tak a thought an' men'!
Ye aiblins might – I dinna ken
    Still hae a stake:
I'm wae to think upo' yon den,
    Ev'n for your sake!

TERMS [Pp36–37] deil – devil; **auld** – old; **clootie** – cloven-footed; **wha** – who; **yon** – that; **spairges** – splashes; **brunstane cootie** – brimstone dish; **scaud** – scald; **hangie** – hangman; **wee** – moment; **sma'** – small; **gie** – give; **skelp** – slap, smack; **kend** – known; **lowan heugh** – blazing hollow; **hame** – home; **lag** – backward; **blate** – bashful; **scaur** – afraid; **whyles** – sometimes; **a'** – all; **tirlan** – stripping, unroofing; **kirks** – churches; **graunie** – grannie; **lanely** – lonely; **eldritch croon** – unearthly moan; **douce** – gentle, respectable; **aft** – often; **yont the dyke** – beyond the wall; **bumman** – humming, droning; **boortries** – elder trees; **coman** – coming

[Pp37–39] ae – one; **sklentan** – slanting; **gat** – got; **ayont** – beyond; **lough** – loch, pond; **rash-buss** – clump of rushes; **sugh** – moan; **nieve** – fist; **stoor** – harsh; **amang** – among; **awa ye squatter'd** – away you flapped; **muirs** – moors; **owre** – over; **howket** – dug up; **countra** – country; **kirn** – churn; **dawtit** – petted; **twal-pint** – twelve-pint; **Hawkie** – name given to a cow; **as yell 's the bill** – as dry as the bull;

guidmen – husbands; **croose** – over-confident; **warklum** – work-tool; **cantraip** – magic; **at the bit** – at the critical moment; **thowes** – thaws; **snawy hoord** – snowy hoard; **boord** – surface; **water-kelpies** – horse-like water spirits; **foord** – ford; **aft** – often; **moss** – bog; **spunkies** – demons; **wight** – fellow; **bleezan** – blazing; **miry slough** – muddy hollow; **ne'er mair** – never more; **maun** – must; **aff** – off; **straught** – straight

[Pp39–41] **lang syne** – long ago; **bonie yard** – lovely garden; **swaird** – sward; **auld** – old; **snick-drawing** – crafty, scheming; **cam** – came; **incog** – incognito, disguised; **brogue** – trick; **fa'** – fall; **gied** – gave; **warld** – world; **shog** – shake; **'maist** – almost; **a'** – all; **mind** – remember; **bizz** – bustle; **reeket duds** – smoky clothes; **reestet gizz** – scorched wig; **smoutie phiz** – smutty face; **'mang** – among; **sklented** – played; **man of Uzz** – Job; **gat** – got; **brak** – broke; **house an' hal'** – house and home; **botches** – sores; **lows'd** – loosed; **scawl** – scold; **warst ava** – worst of all; **fechtin** – fighting; **sin'** – since; **wad ding** – would be beyond the power of; **Lallan** – Lowland Scots ; **Erse** – Scottish Gaelic; **ken** – know; **linkan** – hurrying; **jinkan** – dodging; **men'** – mend; **aiblins** – perhaps; **dinna ken** – don't know; **hae** – have; **wae** – sad; **yon** – that

Tam o' Shanter,
A Tale

Of Brownyis and of Bogillis full is this Buke.
– Gawin Douglas

When chapman billies leave the street,
And drouthy neebors, neebors meet,
As market-days are wearing late,
An' folk begin to tak the gate;
While we sit bousing at the nappy,
And getting fou and unco happy,
We think na on the lang Scots miles,
The mosses, waters, slaps, and styles,
That lie between us and our hame,
Whare sits our sulky, sullen dame,
Gathering her brows like gathering storm,
Nursing her wrath to keep it warm.

This truth fand honest Tam o' Shanter,
As he frae Ayr ae night did canter
(Auld Ayr, wham ne'er a town surpasses,
For honest men and bonie lasses).

O Tam! had'st thou but been sae wise,
As ta'en thy ain wife Kate's advice!
She tauld thee weel thou was a skellum,
A blethering, blustering, drunken blellum;

That frae November till October,
Ae market-day thou was nae sober;
That ilka melder, wi' the miller,
Thou sat as lang as thou had siller;
That ev'ry naig was ca'd a shoe on,
The Smith and thee gat roaring fou on;
That at the Lord's house, even on Sunday,
Thou drank wi' Kirkton Jean till Monday.
She prophesied that, late or soon,
Thou wad be found deep drown'd in Doon,
Or catch'd wi' warlocks in the mirk,
By Alloway's auld, haunted kirk.

Ah, gentle dames! it gars me greet,
To think how mony counsels sweet,
How mony lengthen'd, sage advices,
The husband frae the wife despises!

But to our tale:– Ae market night,
Tam had got planted unco right;
Fast by an ingle, bleezing finely,
Wi' reaming swats, that drank divinely;
And at his elbow, Souter Johnny,
His ancient, trusty, drouthy crony;
Tam lo'ed him like a vera brither –
They had been fou for weeks thegither.
The night drave on wi' sangs an' clatter;
And ay the ale was growing better:

The landlady and Tam grew gracious,
Wi' favours, secret, sweet, and precious:
The Souter tauld his queerest stories;
The landlord's laugh was ready chorus:
The storm without might rair and rustle,
Tam did na mind the storm a whistle.

Care, mad to see a man sae happy,
E'en drown'd himsel amang the nappy:
As bees flee hame wi' lades o' treasure,
The minutes wing'd their way wi' pleasure:
Kings may be blest, but Tam was glorious,
O'er a' the ills o' life victorious!

But pleasures are like poppies spread,
You seize the flower, its bloom is shed;
Or like the snow falls in the river,
A moment white – then melts for ever;
Or like the borealis race,
That flit ere you can point their place;
Or like the rainbow's lovely form
Evanishing amid the storm. –
Nae man can tether time or tide;
The hour approaches Tam maun ride;
That hour, o' night's black arch the key-stane,
That dreary hour he mounts his beast in;
And sic a night he taks the road in,
As ne'er poor sinner was abroad in.

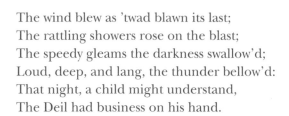

The wind blew as 'twad blawn its last;
The rattling showers rose on the blast;
The speedy gleams the darkness swallow'd;
Loud, deep, and lang, the thunder bellow'd:
That night, a child might understand,
The Deil had business on his hand.

Weel mounted on his gray mare Meg,
A better never lifted leg,
Tam skelpit on thro' dub and mire,
Despising wind, and rain, and fire;
Whiles holding fast his guid blue bonnet;
Whyles crooning o'er some auld Scots sonnet;
Whyles glow'rin round wi' prudent cares,
Lest bogles catch him unawares:
Kirk-Alloway was drawing nigh,
Whare ghaists and houlets nightly cry. –

By this time he was cross the ford,
Whare in the snaw the chapman smoor'd;
And past the birks and meikle stane,
Whare drunken Charlie brak's neck-bane;
And thro' the whins, and by the cairn,
Whare hunters fand the murder'd bairn;
And near the thorn, aboon the well,
Whare Mungo's mither hang'd hersel. –
Before him Doon pours all his floods;
The doubling storm roars thro' the woods;

The lightnings flash from pole to pole;
Near and more near the thunders roll:
When, glimmering thro' the groaning trees,
Kirk-Alloway seem'd in a bleeze,
Thro' ilka bore the beams were glancing;
And loud resounded mirth and dancing.

Inspiring bold John Barleycorn!
What dangers thou canst make us scorn!
Wi' tippenny, we fear nae evil;
Wi' usquabae, we'll face the devil! –
The swats sae ream'd in Tammie's noddle,
Fair play, he car'd na deils a boddle.
But Maggie stood, right sair astonish'd,
Till, by the heel and hand admonish'd,
She ventur'd forward on the light;
And, vow! Tam saw an unco sight!
Warlocks and witches in a dance;
Nae cotillion, brent new frae France,
But hornpipes, jigs, strathspeys, and reels,
Put life and mettle in their heels.
A winnock-bunker in the east,
There sat auld Nick, in shape o' beast;
A towzie tyke, black, grim, and large,
To gie them music was his charge:
He screw'd the pipes and gart them skirl,
Till roof and rafters a' did dirl. –
Coffins stood round, like open presses,

That shaw'd the dead in their last dresses;
And by some devilish cantraip sleight
Each in its cauld hand held a light. –
By which heroic Tam was able
To note upon the haly table,
A murderer's banes, in gibbet-airns;
Twa span-lang, wee, unchristened bairns;
A thief, new-cutted frae a rape,
Wi' his last gasp his gab did gape;
Five tomahawks, wi' blude red-rusted;
Five scymitars, wi' murder crusted;
A garter, which a babe had strangled;
A knife, a father's throat had mangled,
Whom his ain son of life bereft,
The grey-hairs yet stack to the heft;
Wi' mair o' horrible and awfu',
Which even to name wad be unlawfu'.

As Tammie glowr'd, amaz'd, and curious,
The mirth and fun grew fast and furious:
The piper loud and louder blew;
The dancers quick and quicker flew;
They reel'd, they set, they cross'd, they cleekit,
Till ilka carlin swat and reekit,
And coost her duddies to the wark,
And linket at it in her sark!

Now, Tam, O Tam! had thae been queans,

A' plump and strapping in their teens,
Their sarks, instead o' creeshie flannen,
Been snaw-white seventeen hunder linen!
Thir breeks o' mine, my only pair,
That ance were plush o' guid blue hair,
I wad hae gi'en them off my hurdies,
For ae blink o' the bonie burdies!

But wither'd beldams, auld and droll,
Rigwoodie hags wad spean a foal,
Louping and flinging on a crummock,
I wonder did na turn thy stomach.

But Tam kend what was what fu' brawlie:
There was ae winsome wench and wawlie,
That night enlisted in the core,
Lang after kend on Carrick shore;
(For mony a beast to dead she shot,
And perish'd mony a bonie boat,
And shook baith meikle corn and bear,
And kept the country-side in fear).
Her cutty sark, o' Paisley harn,
That while a lassie she had worn,
In longitude tho' sorely scanty,
It was her best, and she was vauntie. –
Ah! little kend thy reverend grannie,
That sark she coft for her wee Nannie,
Wi' twa pund Scots ('twas a' her riches),

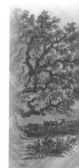

Wad ever grac'd a dance of witches!

But here my Muse her wing maun cour,
Sic flights are far beyond her pow'r;
To sing how Nannie lap and flang
(A souple jade she was, and strang),
And how Tam stood, like ane bewitch'd,
And thought his very een enrich'd;
Even Satan glowr'd, and fidg'd fu' fain,
And hotch'd and blew wi' might and main:
Till first ae caper, syne anither,
Tam tint his reason a' thegither,
And roars out, 'Weel done, Cutty-sark!'
And in an instant all was dark:
And scarcely had he Maggie rallied,
When out the hellish legion sallied.

As bees bizz out wi' angry fyke,
When plundering herds assail their byke;
As open pussie's mortal foes,
When, pop! she starts before their nose;
As eager runs the market-crowd,
When 'Catch the thief!' resounds aloud;
So Maggie runs, the witches follow,
Wi' mony an eldritch skreich and hollow.

Ah, Tam! Ah, Tam! thou'll get thy fairin'!
In hell they'll roast thee like a herrin'!

In vain thy Kate awaits thy comin'!
Kate soon will be a woefu' woman!
Now, do thy speedy utmost, Meg,
And win the key-stane of the brig;
There, at them thou thy tail may toss,
A running stream they dare na cross.
But ere the key-stane she could make,
The fient a tail she had to shake!
For Nannie, far before the rest,
Hard upon noble Maggie prest,
And flew at Tam wi' furious ettle;
But little wist she Maggie's mettle! –
Ae spring brought off her master hale,
But left behind her ain grey tail:
The carlin claught her by the rump,
And left poor Maggie scarce a stump.

Now, wha this tale o' truth shall read,
Ilk man and mother's son, take heed:
Whene'er to drink you are inclin'd,
Or cutty-sarks rin in your mind,
Think! ye may buy the joys o'er dear:
Remember Tam o' Shanter's mare.

TERMS [Pp43–44] bogillis – ghosts, apparitions; **chapman billies** – pedlar friends; **drouthy neebors** – thirsty neighbours; **tak the gate** – set off home; **bousing** – drinking; **nappy** – strong ale; **fou** – drunk; **unco** – very; **na** – not; **lang** – long; **mosses** – marshes, moorland; **waters** –

streams; **slaps** – gaps in walls or hedges; **hame** – home; **fand** – found; **ae** – one; **bonie** – pretty; **sae** – so; **as ta'en** – as to have taken; **ain** – own; **tauld** – told; **skellum** – rogue; **blethering** – prattling; **blellum** – babbler; **nae** – not; **ilka melder** – every milling; **siller** – money; **naig** – horse; **ca'd a shoe on** – shoed; **catch'd wi'** – caught by; **mirk** – darkness; **kirk** – church; **gars me greet** – makes me weep; **mony** – many; **frae** – from

[Pp44–46] **ingle** – fireplace; **reaming swats** – foaming beer; **souter** – cobbler; **drouthy** – thirsty; **lo'ed** – loved; **a vera brither** – a real brother; **thegither** – together; **drave** – drove; **sangs** – songs; **clatter** – chatter; **ay** – always; **tauld** – told; **rair** – roar; **na** – not; **flee hame** – fly home; **lades** – loads; **a'** – all; **nae** – no; **maun** – must; **stane** – stone; **sic** – such; **taks** – takes; **as 'twad blawn** – as if it would have blown; **Deil** – Devil

[Pp46–48] **weel** – well; **skelpit** – galloped; **dub** – puddle; **whyles ... whyles ...** – now ... now ...; **glow'rin** – looking; **bogles** – ghosts; **ghaists and houlets** – ghosts and owls; **cross** – across; **snaw** – snow; **the chapman smoor'd** – the pedlar suffocated; **birks** – birch trees; **meikle stane** – big stone; **brak** – broke; **bane** – bone; **whins** – gorse bushes; **fand** – found; **bairn** – child; **thorn** – hawthorn; **aboon** – above; **mither** – mother; **in a bleeze** – ablaze, lit up; **ilka bore** – every chink; **tippenny** – ale; **usquabae** – whisky; **the swats sae ream'd** – the beer frothed so much; **noddle** – head; **he car'd na deils a boddle** – he didn't care a farthing for devils; **sair** – sorely, very; **unco** – strange; **brent new frae** – brand new from; **winnock-bunker** – window recess; **towzie tyke** – shaggy dog; **gie** – give; **gart them skirl** – made them squeal; **a'** – all; **dirl** – ring; **presses** – cupboards; **shaw'd** – showed; **cantraip sleight** – magic trick; **cauld** – cold; **haly** – holy; **banes** – bones; **airns** – irons; **twa** – two; **span-lang** – a span-long; **bairns** – children; **rape** – rope; **gab** – mouth; **ain** – own; **stack** – stuck; **mair** – more; **glowr'd** – stared; **cleekit** – linked arms; **ilka carlin** – every witch; **swat and reekit** – sweated and steamed; **coost her duddies**

– threw off her ragged clothes; **wark** – work; **linket at it** – skipped and danced; **sark** – chemise

[Pp48–50] thae – those; **queans** – girls; **creeshie flannen** – greasy flannel; **seventeen hunder linen** – fine linen; **thir breeks** – these trousers; **ance** – once; **guid** – good; **gi'en** – given; **hurdies** – buttocks; **ae blink** – one glimpse; **bonie burdies** – lovely girls; **beldams** – hags; **auld** – old; **rigwoodie** – wizened; **wad spean a foal** – that would suckle (or possibly abort) a foal; **louping** – leaping; **crummock** – stick, crook; **kend** – knew; **fu' brawlie** – very well; **wawlie** – fine, jolly, agile; **core** – party, company; **mony** – many; **dead** – death; **perish'd** – destroyed; **baith** – both; **meikle** – much; **bear** – barley; **cutty sark** – short chemise; **harn** – coarse cloth; **vauntie** – proud; **coft** – bought; **twa pund Scots** – two Scots pounds; **wad ever grac'd** – would ever have graced; **maun cour** – must curb; **sic** – such; **lap and flang** – leaped and capered; **souple jade** – supple lass; **strang** – strong; **een** – eyes; **glowr'd** – stared; **fidg'd fu' fain** – wriggled in excitement; **hotch'd** – jerked; **syne** – then; **tint** – lost; **a' thegither** – altogether

[Pp50–51] fyke – fuss, commotion; **byke** – nest; **pussie** – hare; **mony** – many; **eldritch skreich** – unearthly screech; **get thy fairin'** – get what's coming to you; **the key-stane of the brig** – the key-stone of the bridge; **na** – not; **the fient a tail** – not a bit of a tail; **ettle** – purpose; **wist** – knew; **hale** – whole, uninjured; **ain** – own; **carlin** – witch; **claught** – caught hold of; **ilk** – each; **rin** – run

Address to the Unco Guid, or the Rigidly Righteous

My Son, these maxims make a rule,
An' lump them ay thegither;
The Rigid Righteous is a fool,
The Rigid Wise anither:
The cleanest corn that e'er was dight
May hae some pyles o' caff in;
So ne'er a fellow-creature slight
For random fits o' daffin.
Solomon (Eccles. ch. vii. verse 16)

O ye wha are sae guid yoursel,
Sae pious and sae holy,
Ye've nought to do but mark and tell
Your Neebours' fauts and folly!
Whase life is like a weel-gaun mill,
Supplied wi' store o' water;
The heapet happer's ebbing still,
An' still the clap plays clatter.

Hear me, ye venerable Core,
As counsel for poor mortals,
That frequent pass douce Wisdom's door
For glaikit Folly's portals;
I, for their thoughtless, careless sakes,
Would here propone defences,

Their donsie tricks, their black mistakes,
Their failings and mischances.

Ye see your state wi' theirs compared,
And shudder at the niffer,
But cast a moment's fair regard,
What maks the mighty differ;
Discount what scant occasion gave,
That purity ye pride in,
And (what's aft mair than a' the lave),
Your better art o' hidin.

Think, when your castigated pulse
Gies now and then a wallop,
What ragings must his veins convulse,
That still eternal gallop:
Wi' wind and tide fair i' your tail,
Right on ye scud your sea-way;
But in the teeth o' baith to sail,
It maks an unco leeway.

See Social-life and Glee sit down,
All joyous and unthinking,
Till, quite transmugrify'd, they're grown
Debauchery and Drinking:
O, would they stay to calculate
Th' eternal consequences;
Or your more dreaded hell to state,
Damnation of expenses!

Ye high, exalted, virtuous Dames,
Ty'd up in godly laces,
Before ye gie poor Frailty names,
Suppose a change o' cases;
A dear-lov'd lad, convenience snug,
A treach'rous inclination –
But, let me whisper i' your lug,
Ye're aiblins nae temptation.

Then gently scan your brother Man,
Still gentler sister Woman;
Tho' they may gang a kennin wrang,
To step aside is human:
One point must still be greatly dark,
The moving *Why* they do it;
And just as lamely can ye mark,
How far perhaps they rue it.

Who made the heart, 'tis He alone
Decidedly can try us;
He knows each chord its various tone,
Each spring its various bias:
Then at the balance let's be mute,
We never can adjust it;
What's *done* we partly may compute,
But know not what's *resisted*.

TERMS **the unco guid** – the extremely/excessively good; **ay thegither** – always together; **anither** – another; **dight** – sifted; **hae** – have; **pyles o' caff** – odd pieces of chaff; **daffin** – fun, foolish behaviour; **wha** – who; **sae** – so; **neebours' fauts** – neighbours' faults; **whase** – whose; **weel-gaun** – well-going; **heapet happer** – heaped hopper; **clap** – device for shaking a hopper; **core** – crowd, company; **douce** – sober, respectable; **glaikit** – foolish; **propone** – propose, put forward in a court of law; **donsie** – unlucky, stupid; **niffer** – comparison; **maks** – makes; **aft** – often; **mair** – more; **a' the lave** – all the rest; **gies** – gives; **scud** – move fast; **baith** – both; **unco** – uncommon; **ty'd** – tied; **gie** – give; **lug** – ear; **aiblins** – perhaps; **nae** – no; **gang a kennin wrang** – go a little wrong

Holy Willie's Prayer

O Thou that in the Heavens does dwell!
Wha, as it pleases best Thysel,
Sends ane to Heaven an' ten to Hell,
    A' for Thy glory!
And no for ony guid or ill
    They've done before Thee.

I bless and praise Thy matchless might,
When thousands Thou hast left in night,
That I am here afore Thy sight,
    For gifts an' grace
A burning and a shining light
    To a' this place.

What was I, or my generation,
That I should get sic exaltation?
I, wha deserve most just damnation
     For broken laws
Sax thousand years ere my creation,
     Thro' Adam's cause!

When from my mither's womb I fell,
Thou might hae plunged me deep in hell,
To gnash my gooms, and weep, and wail,
     In burning lakes,
Whare damned devils roar and yell,
     Chain'd to their stakes.

Yet I am here, a chosen sample,
To show Thy grace is great and ample:
I'm here a pillar o' Thy temple,
     Strong as a rock,
A guide, a ruler and example,
     To a' Thy flock.

O Lord, Thou kens what zeal I bear,
When drinkers drink, an' swearers swear,
An' singin' there, an' dancin' here,
     Wi' great and sma';
For I am keepet by Thy fear,
     Free frae them a'.

But yet, O Lord! confess I must,
At times I'm fash'd wi' fleshly lust;
An' sometimes, too, in warldly trust,
    Vile Self gets in:
But Thou remembers we are dust,
    Defil'd wi' sin.

O Lord! – yestreen – Thou kens – wi' Meg –
Thy pardon I sincerely beg!
O! may't ne'er be a living plague
    To my dishonour!
An' I'll ne'er lift a lawless leg
    Again upon her.

Besides, I farther maun avow,
Wi' Leezie's lass, three times – I trow –
But Lord, that Friday I was fou,
    When I cam near her;
Or else, Thou kens, Thy servant true
    Wad never steer her.

Maybe Thou lets this fleshly thorn
Buffet Thy servant e'en and morn,
Lest he owre proud and high should turn,
    That he's sae gifted:
If sae, Thy han' maun e'en be borne,
    Until Thou lift it.

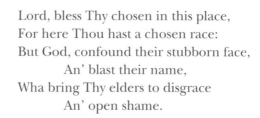

Lord, bless Thy chosen in this place,
For here Thou hast a chosen race:
But God, confound their stubborn face,
      An' blast their name,
Wha bring Thy elders to disgrace
      An' open shame.

Lord, mind Gaun Hamilton's deserts!
He drinks, an' swears, an' plays at cartes,
Yet has sae monie takin arts,
      Wi' Great and Sma',
Frae God's ain priest the people's hearts
      He steals awa.

An' when we chasten'd him therefore,
Thou kens how he bred sic a splore,
An' set the warld in a roar
      O' laughing at us:
Curse Thou his basket and his store,
      Kail an' potatoes.

Lord, hear my earnest cry and pray'r,
Against that Presbytry o' Ayr!
Thy strong right hand, Lord, make it bare
      Upon their heads!
Lord visit them, an' dinna spare,
      For their misdeeds.

O Lord, my God, that glib-tongu'd Aiken!
My vera heart and flesh are quaking,
To think how I sat, sweating, shaking,
   An' pish'd wi' dread,
While he, wi' hingin lip an' snakin,
   Held up his head!

Lord, in Thy day o' vengeance try him!
Lord, visit them wha did employ him!
And pass not in Thy mercy by them,
   Nor hear their prayer,
But for Thy people's sake destroy them,
   An' dinna spare.

But, Lord, remember me an' mine
Wi' mercies temporal an' divine,
That I for grace an' gear may shine,
   Excell'd by nane,
And a' the glory shall be Thine!
   Amen, Amen!

TERMS ane – one; **no** – not; **sic** – such; **sax** – six; **gooms** – gums; **sma'** –
small; **kens** – know; **keepet** – kept; **fash'd** – troubled; **warldly** – worldly;
yestreen – last night; **maun** – must; **trow** – think; **fou** – drunk; **cam** – came;
wad never steer her – would never molest her; **e'en** – evening; **owre**
– too; **if sae** – if so; **han'** – hand; **e'en** – even; **mind** – remember; **sae
monie takin arts** – so many taking/popular ways; **ain** – own; **splore** – row,

commotion; **kail** – cabbage; **dinna** – do not; **vera** – very; **pish'd** – wet myself; **hingin** – hanging; **snakin** – sneering; **gear** – wealth; **nane** – none

 ## Epitaph on Holy Willie

Here Holy Willie's sair worn clay
Taks up its last abode;
His saul has ta'en some other way,
I fear, the left-hand road.

Stop! there he is, as sure's a gun,
Poor, silly body, see him;
Nae wonder he's as black's the grun,
Observe wha's standing wi' him.

Your brunstane devilship, I see,
Has got him there before ye;
But haud your nine-tail cat a wee,
Till ance you've heard my story.

Your pity I will not implore,
For pity ye have nane;
Justice, alas! has gi'en him o'er,
And mercy's day is gaen.

But hear me, Sir, deil as ye are,
Look something to your credit;

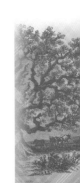

A coof like him wad stain your name,
If it were kent ye did it.

TERMS sair – sorely, very; **taks** – takes; **nae** – no; **grun** – ground;
brunstane – brimstone; **haud** – hold back; **a wee** – a moment; **ance** – once;
gi'en – given; **gaen** – gone; **deil** – devil; **coof** – fool, rogue; **kent** – known

Address to Edinburgh

Edina! Scotia's darling seat!
All hail thy palaces and tow'rs,
Where once beneath a Monarch's feet,
Sat Legislation's sov'reign pow'rs!
From marking wildly-scatt'red flow'rs,
As on the banks of Ayr I stray'd,
And singing, lone, the ling'ring hours,
I shelter in thy honor'd shade.

Here Wealth still swells the golden tide,
As busy Trade his labours plies;
There Architecture's noble pride
Bids elegance and splendour rise;
Here Justice, from her native skies,
High wields her balance and her rod;
There Learning, with his eagle eyes,
Seeks Science in her coy abode.

Thy sons, Edina, social, kind,
With open arms the Stranger hail;
Their views enlarg'd, their liberal mind,
Above the narrow, rural vale:
Attentive still to Sorrow's wail,
Or modest Merit's silent claim;
And never may their sources fail!
And never Envy blot their name!

Thy daughters bright thy walks adorn,
Gay as the gilded summer sky,
Sweet as the dewy, milk-white thorn,
Dear as the raptur'd thrill of joy!
Fair Burnet strikes th' adoring eye,
Heav'n's beauties on my fancy shine;
I see the Sire of Love on high,
And own His work indeed divine!

There, watching high the least alarms,
Thy rough, rude Fortress gleams afar;
Like some bold Vet'ran, grey in arms,
And mark'd with many a seamy scar:
The pond'rous wall and massy bar,
Grim-rising o'er the rugged rock,
Have oft withstood assailing War,
And oft repell'd th' Invader's shock.

With awe-struck thought, and pitying tears,
I view that noble, stately Dome,
Where Scotia's kings of other years,
Fam'd heroes! had their royal home:
Alas, how chang'd the times to come!
Their royal Name low in the dust!
Their hapless Race wild-wand'ring roam!
Tho' rigid Law cries out, 'twas just!

Wild-beats my heart, to trace your steps,
Whose ancestors, in days of yore,
Thro' hostile ranks and ruin'd gaps
Old Scotia's bloody lion bore:
Ev'n I who sing in rustic lore,
Haply my Sires have left their shed,
And fac'd grim Danger's loudest roar,
Bold-following where your Fathers led!

Edina! Scotia's darling seat!
All hail thy palaces and tow'rs;
Where once, beneath a Monarch's feet,
Sat Legislation's sovereign pow'rs!
From marking wildly-scatt'red flow'rs,
As on the banks of Ayr I stray'd,
And singing, lone, the ling'ring hours,
I shelter in thy honour'd shade.

TERMS thorn – hawthorn

 ## Mary Morison

O Mary, at thy window be,
It is the wish'd, the trysted hour;
Those smiles and glances let me see,
That make the miser's treasure poor:
How blythely wad I bide the stour,
A weary slave frae sun to sun,
Could I the rich reward secure,
The lovely Mary Morison.

Yestreen when to the trembling string
The dance gaed thro' the lighted ha',
To thee my fancy took its wing,
I sat, but neither heard nor saw:
Though this was fair, and that was braw,
And yon the toast of a' the town,
I sigh'd, and said amang them a',
'Ye are na Mary Morison.'

Oh, Mary, canst thou wreck his peace,
Wha for thy sake wad gladly die?
Or canst thou break that heart of his,
Whase only faut is loving thee?
If love for love thou wilt na gie,
At least be pity to me shown;
A thought ungentle canna be
The thought o' Mary Morison.

TERMS blythely – cheerfully; **wad** – would; **bide the stour** – put up
with the struggle; **frae** – from; **yestreen** – last night; **gaed** – went;
ha' – hall; **braw** – pretty; **yon** – that one; **a'** – all; **amang** – among;
na – not; **wha** – who; **whase** – whose; **faut** – fault; **gie** – give;
canna – cannot

Ae Fond Kiss

Ae fond kiss, and then we sever;
Ae fareweel, and then for ever!
Deep in heart-wrung tears I'll pledge thee,
Warring sighs and groans I'll wage thee.

Who shall say that Fortune grieves him,
While the star of hope she leaves him?
Me, nae cheerfu' twinkle lights me;
Dark despair around benights me.

I'll ne'er blame my partial fancy,
Naething could resist my Nancy:
But to see her, was to love her;
Love but her, and love for ever.

Had we never lov'd sae kindly,
Had we never lov'd sae blindly,

Never met – or never parted,
We had ne'er been broken-hearted.

Fare-thee-weel, thou first and fairest!
Fare-thee-weel, thou best and dearest!
Thine be ilka joy and treasure,
Peace, Enjoyment, Love and Pleasure!

Ae fond kiss, and then we sever!
Ae fareweel, Alas, for ever!
Deep in heart-wrung tears I'll pledge thee,
Warring sighs and groans I'll wage thee.

TERMS ae – one; **wage** – pledge; **nae** – no; **naething** – nothing;
sae – so; **ilka** – every

My Luve is like a Red, Red Rose

O my Luve is like a red, red rose,
That's newly sprung in June;
O my Luve is like the melodie
That's sweetly play'd in tune.

As fair art thou, my bonie lass,
So deep in luve am I;
And I will luve thee still, my Dear,
Till a' the seas gang dry.

Till a' the seas gang dry, my Dear,
And the rocks melt wi' the sun:
I will luve thee still, my Dear,
While the sands o' life shall run.

And fare thee weel, my only Luve!
And fare thee weel, a while!
And I will come again, my Luve,
Tho' it were ten thousand mile!

TERMS bonie – pretty; **a'** – all; **gang** – go; **weel** – well

Sweet Afton

Flow gently, sweet Afton, among thy green
    braes,
Flow gently, I'll sing thee a song in thy praise;
My Mary's asleep by thy murmuring stream,
Flow gently, sweet Afton, disturb not her dream.

Thou stock dove whose echo resounds thro' the
    glen,
Ye wild whistling blackbirds in yon thorny den,
Thou green-crested lapwing, thy screaming
    forbear,
I charge you, disturb not my slumbering Fair.

How lofty, sweet Afton, thy neighbouring hills,
Far mark'd with the courses of clear, winding
    rills;
There daily I wander as noon rises high,
My flocks and my Mary's sweet Cot in my eye.

How pleasant thy banks and green vallies below,
Where wild in the woodlands the primroses
    blow;
There oft, as mild ev'ning weeps over the lea,
The sweet-scented birk shades my Mary and me.

Thy chrystal stream, Afton, how lovely it glides,

And winds by the cot where my Mary resides;
How wanton thy waters her snowy feet lave,
As, gathering sweet flowerets, she stems thy
clear wave.

Flow gently, sweet Afton, among thy green
braes,
Flow gently, sweet River, the theme of my lays;
My Mary's asleep by thy murmuring stream,
Flow gently, sweet Afton, disturb not her
dream.

TERMS braes – slopes, hillsides; **yon** – that; **cot** – cottage; **birk** –
birch tree; **lave** – wash

John Anderson My Jo

John Anderson my jo, John,
When we were first acquent,
Your locks were like the raven,
Your bonie brow was brent;
But now your brow is beld, John,
Your locks are like the snaw;
But blessings on your frosty pow,
John Anderson my jo.

John Anderson my jo, John,
We clamb the hill thegither;
And mony a cantie day, John,
We've had wi' ane anither:
Now we maun totter down, John,
And hand in hand we'll go,
And sleep thegither at the foot,
John Anderson my jo.

TERMS jo – darling; **acquent** – acquainted; **bonie** – handsome, fair;
brent – smooth; **beld** – bald; **snaw** – snow; **pow** – head; **clamb** –
climbed; **thegither** – together; **mony a cantie day** – many a happy day;
ane anither – one another; **maun** – must

Highland Mary

Ye banks, and braes, and streams around
The castle o' Montgomery,
Green be your woods, and fair your flowers,
Your waters never drumlie!
There Simmer first unfald her robes,
And there the langest tarry:
For there I took the last Fareweel
O' my sweet Highland Mary.

How sweetly bloom'd the gay, green birk,
How rich the hawthorn's blossom,
As underneath their fragrant shade,
I clasp'd her to my bosom!
The golden Hours on angel wings,
Flew o'er me and my Dearie;
For dear to me as light and life
Was my sweet Highland Mary.

Wi' monie a vow, and lock'd embrace,
Our parting was fu' tender;
And, pledging aft to meet again,
We tore oursels asunder;
But Oh! fell Death's untimely frost,
That nipt my Flower sae early!
Now green's the sod, and cauld's the clay
That wraps my Highland Mary!

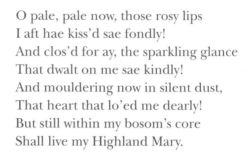

Highland Mary

O pale, pale now, those rosy lips
I aft hae kiss'd sae fondly!
And clos'd for ay, the sparkling glance
That dwalt on me sae kindly!
And mouldering now in silent dust,
That heart that lo'ed me dearly!
But still within my bosom's core
Shall live my Highland Mary.

TERMS **braes** – hillsides; **drumlie** – muddy; **simmer** – summer; **unfald**
– unfold; **langest** – longest; **birk** – birch; **monie** – many; **fu'** – very; **aft**
– often; **fell** – cruel; **sae** – so; **cauld** – cold; **hae** – have; **for ay** – forever;
dwalt – dwelt; **lo'ed** – loved

The Banks o' Doon

Ye banks and braes o' bonie Doon,
How can ye bloom sae fresh and fair;
How can ye chant, ye little birds,
And I sae weary, fu' o' care!
Thou'll break my heart, thou warbling bird,
That wantons thro' the flowering thorn:
Thou minds me o' departed joys,
Departed never to return.

Aft hae I rov'd by bonie Doon,
To see the rose and woodbine twine:
And ilka bird sang o' its Luve,
And fondly sae did I o' mine.
Wi' lightsome heart I pu'd a rose,
Fu' sweet upon its thorny tree;
And my fause Luver staw my rose,
But ah! he left the thorn wi' me.

TERMS braes – slopes; **bonie** – lovely; **sae** – so; **fu'** – full; **minds** –
remind; **aft** – often; **hae** – have; **ilka** – every; **pu'd** – pulled;
fu' – very; **fause** – false; **staw** – stole

A Rosebud by My Early Walk

A Rosebud by my early walk,
Adown a corn-enclosed bawk,
Sae gently bent its thorny stalk,
All on a dewy morning.

Ere twice the shades o' dawn are fled,
In a' its crimson glory spread,
And drooping rich the dewy head,
It scents the early morning.

Within the bush her covert nest
A little linnet fondly prest;
The dew sat chilly on her breast,
Sae early in the morning.

She soon shall see her tender brood,
The pride, the pleasure o' the wood,
Amang the fresh green leaves bedew'd,
Awauk the early morning.

So thou, dear bird, young Jeany fair,
On trembling string or vocal air,
Shall sweetly pay the tender care
That tents thy early morning.

So thou, sweet Rosebud, young and gay,
Shalt beauteous blaze upon the day,
And bless the Parent's evening ray
That watch'd thy early morning.

TERMS bawk – strip of unploughed land; **sae** – so; **a'** – all; **amang** –
among; **awauk** – awake; **tents** – tends, guards

The Birks of Aberfeldey

Now Simmer blinks on flowery braes,
And o'er the chrystal streamlets plays;
Come let us spend the lightsome days,
In the birks of Aberfeldey.

Chorus
Bonie lassie, will ye go,
Will ye go, will ye go,
Bonie lassie, will ye go
To the birks of Aberfeldey?

The little birdies blythely sing,
While o'er their heads the hazels hing,
Or lightly flit on wanton wing
In the birks of Aberfeldey.

The braes ascend like lofty wa's,
The foaming stream deep-roaring fa's,
O'erhung wi' fragrant-spreading shaws,
The birks of Aberfeldey.

The hoary cliffs are crown'd wi' flowers,
White o'er the linns the burnie pours,
And, rising, weets wi' misty showers
The birks of Aberfeldey.

Let Fortune's gifts at random flee,
They ne'er shall draw a wish frae me,
Supremely blest wi' love and thee
In the birks of Aberfeldey.

TERMS **simmer** – summer; **braes** – hillsides; **birks** – birch trees; **bonie** – lovely; **blythely** – cheerfully; **hing** – hang; **wa's** – walls; **fa's** – falls; **shaws** – thickets; **linns** – waterfalls; **burnie** – stream; **weets** – wets; **frae** – from

O Wert Thou in the Cauld Blast

O wert thou in the cauld blast,
On yonder lea, on yonder lea,
My plaidie to the angry airt,
I'd shelter thee, I'd shelter thee:
Or did Misfortune's bitter storms
Around thee blaw, around thee blaw,
Thy bield should be my bosom,
To share it a', to share it a'.

Or were I in the wildest waste,
Sae black and bare, sae black and bare,
The desert were a Paradise,
If thou wert there, if thou wert there:
Or were I monarch o' the globe,
Wi' thee to reign, wi' thee to reign,
The brightest jewel in my crown
Wad be my queen, wad be my queen.

TERMS cauld – cold; **plaidie** – plaid; **airt** – direction (of the wind);
blaw – blow; **bield** – shelter; **a'** – all; **sae** – so; **wad** — would

O Whistle, an' I'll Come to Ye, My Lad

Chorus
O whistle, an' I'll come to ye, my lad,
O whistle, an' I'll come to ye, my lad;
Tho' father an' mother an' a' should gae mad,
Thy Jeanie will venture wi' ye, my lad.

But warily tent, when ye come to court me,
And come nae unless the back-yett be a-jee;
Syne up the back-style, and let naebody see,
And come as ye were na comin to me
And come as ye were na comin to me.

At kirk, or at market, whene'er ye meet me,
Gang by me as tho' that ye car'd na a flie;
But steal me a blink o' your bonie black e'e,
Yet look as ye were na lookin to me –
Yet look as ye were na lookin to me.

Ay vow and protest that ye care na for me,
And whyles ye may lightly my beauty a wee;
But court na anither, tho' jokin' ye be,
For fear that she wyle your fancy frae me
For fear that she wyle your fancy frae me.

TERMS a' – all; **gae** – go; **tent** – take care; **nae** – not; **yett** – gate; **a-jee** – ajar; **syne** – then; **style** – stile; **naebody** – nobody; **na** – not; **kirk** – church; **gang** – go; **car'd na a flie** – cared not a whit; **blink** – glance ; **bonie** – lovely; **e'e** – eye; **ay** – always; **whyles** – now and again; **lightly** – make light of; **a wee** – a little; **anither** – another; **wyle** – lure; **frae** – from

 ## Of a' the Airts

Of a' the airts the wind can blaw,
I dearly like the West,
For there the bonie Lassie lives,
The Lassie I lo'e best:
There's wild-woods grow, and rivers row,
And mony a hill between;
But day and night my fancy's flight
Is ever wi' my Jean.

I see her in the dewy flowers,
I see her sweet and fair;
I hear her in the tunefu' birds,
I hear her charm the air:
There's not a bonie flower that springs
By fountain, shaw, or green;
There's not a bonie bird that sings,
But minds me o' my Jean.

TERMS airts – directions; **blaw** – blow; **bonie** – lovely; **lo'e** – love; **row** – roll, flow; **mony** – many; **shaw** – wood, thicket; **green** – grassy place; **minds** – reminds

Tam Glen

My heart is a breaking, dear Tittie,
Some counsel unto me come len';
To anger them a' is a pity,
But what will I do wi' Tam Glen?

I'm thinking, wi' sic a braw fellow,
In poortith I might mak a fen':
What care I in riches to wallow,
If I mauna marry Tam Glen?

There's Lowrie the laird o' Dumeller –
'Gude day to you, brute!' – he comes ben:
He brags and he blaws o' his siller,
But when will he dance like Tam Glen?

My Minnie does constantly deave me,
And bids me beware o' young men;
They flatter, she says, to deceive me,
But wha can think sae o' Tam Glen?

My Daddie says, gin I'll forsake him,
He'd gie me gude hunder marks ten:
But, if it's ordain'd I maun take him,
O wha will I get but Tam Glen?

Yestreen at the Valentines' dealing,
My heart to my mou gied a sten;
For thrice I drew ane without failing,
And thrice it was written 'Tam Glen'!

The last Halloween I was waukin
My droukit sark-sleeve, as ye ken;
His likeness came up the house staukin,
And the very grey breeks o' Tam Glen!

Come, counsel, dear Tittie, don't tarry;
I'll gie ye my bonie black hen,
Gif ye will advise me to marry
The lad I lo'e dearly, Tam Glen.

TERMS tittie – sister; **len'** – lend; **a'** – all; **sic a braw fellow** – such a fine fellow; **poortith** – poverty; **mak a fen'** – manage; **mauna** – may not; **laird** – landowner; **gude** – good; **ben** – into the parlour; **blaws** – blows, boasts; **siller** – money; **minnie** – mother; **deave** – deafen, irritate with talking; **wha** – who; **sae** – so; **gin** – if; **gie** – give; **hunder marks ten** – a hundred and ten marks (a mark was worth £0.66); **maun** – must; **yestreen** – last night; **mou** – mouth; **gied a sten** – gave a jump; **ane** – one; **waukin my droukit sark-sleeve** – watching my soaking chemise-sleeve; **ken** – know; **breeks** – trousers; **bonie** – pretty; **gif** – if; **lo'e** – love

 My Bonie Mary

Go fetch to me a pint o' wine,
And fill it in a silver tassie;
That I may drink before I go,
A service to my bonie lassie.
The boat rocks at the Pier o' Leith,
Fu' loud the wind blaws frae the Ferry,
The ship rides by the Berwick-law,
And I maun leave my bonie Mary.

The trumpets sound, the banners fly,
The glittering spears are ranked ready,
The shouts o' war are heard afar,
The battle closes deep and bloody.
It's not the roar o' sea or shore,
Wad mak me langer wish to tarry,
Nor shouts o' war that's heard afar
It's leaving thee, my bonie Mary!

TERMS tassie – cup, goblet; **bonie** – lovely; **fu'** – very; **blaws** – blows;
frae – from; **maun** – must; **wad mak** – would make; **langer** – longer

The Country Lassie

In simmer, when the hay was mawn,
And corn wav'd green in ilka field,
While claver blooms white o'er the lea,
And roses blaw in ilka beild;
Blythe Bessie, in the milking shiel,
Says, I'll be wed, come o't what will.
Out spake a dame in wrinkled eild,
O' gude advisement comes nae ill.

It's ye hae wooers mony ane,
And lassie, ye're but young, ye ken;
Then wait a wee, and cannie wale
A routhie butt, a routhie ben:
There's Johnie o' the Buskieglen,
Fu' is his barn, fu' is his byre;
Take this frae me, my bonie hen,
It's plenty beets the luver's fire.

For Johnie o' the Buskieglen,
I dinna care a single flie;
He lo'es sae weel his craps and kye,
He has nae loove to spare for me:
But blythe's the blink o' Robie's e'e,
And weel I wat he lo'es me dear:
Ae blink o' him I wad na gie
For Buskieglen and a' his gear.

O thoughtless lassie, life's a faught,
The canniest gate, the strife is sair;
But aye fu'-han't is fechtin best,
A hungry care's an unco care:
But some will spend and some will spare,
An' wilfu' folk maun hae their will;
Syne as ye brew, my maiden fair,
Keep mind that ye maun drink the yill.

O gear will buy me rigs o' land,
And gear will buy me sheep and kye;
But the tender heart o' leesome loove,
The gowd and siller canna buy:
We may be poor, Robie and I,
Light is the burden Loove lays on;
Content and Loove brings peace and joy,
What mair hae queens upon a throne?

TERMS simmer – summer; **mawn** – mown; **ilka** – every; **claver** – clover;
blaw – blow; **beild** – sheltered spot; **blythe** – cheerful; **shiel** – shed;
o't – of it; **spake** – spoke; **eild** – old age; **gude advisement** – good
advice; **many ane** – many a one; **a wee** – a while; **cannie wale** – chose
carefully; **routhie butt** – well-stocked kitchen; **ben** – parlour; **my bonie
hen** – my lovely girl; **beets** – fans; **dinna care a single flie** – don't care
a whit; **lo'es sae weel** – loves so well; **craps and kye** – crops and cattle;
nae loove – no love; **blink** – glance; **e'e** – eye; **weel I wat** – well I know;
ae – one; **wad na gie** – would not give; **gear** – possessions; **faught** –
struggle; **canniest gate** – most prudent way; **sair** – hard; **fu-han't** – full-

handed; **fechtin** – fighting; **unco** – great; **maun hae** – must have; **syne as ye brew, ye maun drink the yill** – so as you brew, you must drink the ale (= as you make your bed, so you must lie in it); **keep mind** – remember; **rigs** – strips; **leesome** – pleasant; **gowd and siller** – gold and silver; **canna** – cannot; **mair** – more

The Bonie Lass o' Ballochmyle

'Twas ev'n, the dewy fields were green,
On ev'ry blade the pearls hang;
The Zephyr wanton'd round the bean,
And bore its fragrant sweets alang:
In ev'ry glen the Mavis sang,
All Nature list'ning seem'd the while,
Except where greenwood Echoes rang,
Amang the braes o' Ballochmyle.

With careless step I onward stray'd,
My heart rejoic'd in Nature's joy,
When, musing in a lonely glade,
A Maiden fair I chanc'd to spy:
Her look was like the Morning's eye,
Her air like Nature's vernal smile:
The lilies' hue and roses' dye
Bespoke the lass o' Ballochmyle.

Fair is the morn in flow'ry May,
And sweet an ev'n in Autumn mild;
When roving thro' the garden gay,
Or wand'ring in the lonely wild;
But Woman, Nature's darling child,
There all her charms she does compile,
And there her other works are foil'd
By the bonie Lass o' Ballochmyle.

O if she were a country maid,
And I the happy country Swain!
Though shelter'd in the lowest shed
That ever rose on Scotia's plain:
Through weary Winter's wind and rain,
With joy, with rapture, I would toil,
And nightly to my bosom strain
The bonie lass o' Ballochmyle.

Then Pride might climb the slipp'ry steep
Where fame and honours lofty shine;
And Thirst of gold might tempt the deep,
Or downward seek the Indian mine:
Give me the Cot below the pine,
To tend the flocks or till the soil;
And ev'ry day have joys divine
With the bonie Lass o' Ballochmyle.

TERMS hang – hung; **mavis** – song thrush; **braes** – slopes

I'm O'er Young to Marry Yet

I am my mammy's ae bairn,
Wi' unco folk I weary, Sir;
And lying in a man's bed,
I'm fley'd it make me irie, sir.

Chorus
I'm o'er young, I'm o'er young,
I'm o'er young to marry yet;
I'm o'er young, 'twad be a sin
To tak me frae my mammy yet.

Hallowmass is come and gane,
The nights are lang in winter, Sir;
And you an' I in ae bed,
In trowth, I dare na venture, Sir.

Fu' loud an' shill the frosty wind
Blaws thro' the leafless timmer, Sir;
But if ye come this gate again,
I'll aulder be gin simmer, Sir.

TERMS ae bairn – only child; **unco folk** – strangers; **fley'd** – afraid; **irie**
– melancholy; **o'er** – too; **'twad** – it would; **tak** – take; **Hallowmass** – All
Saints' Day; **gane** – gone; **lang** – long; **ae** – one; **trowth** – truth; **na** – not;
fu' – fully, very; **shill** – shrill; **blaws** – blows; **timmer** – trees; **come this
gate** – come this way; **aulder** – older; **gin simmer** – by summer

Duncan Gray

Duncan Gray cam here to woo,
Ha, ha, the wooing o't,
On blythe Yule-night when we were fu',
Ha, ha, the wooing o't.
Maggie coost her head fu' high,
Look'd asklent and unco skeigh,
Gart poor Duncan stand abeigh,
Ha, ha, the wooing o't.

Duncan fleech'd, and Duncan pray'd,
Ha, ha, the wooing o't.
Meg was deaf as Ailsa Craig,
Ha, ha, the wooing o't.
Duncan sigh'd baith out and in,
Grat his een baith bleer't an' blin',
Spak o' lowpin o'er a linn;
Ha, ha, the wooing o't.

Time and Chance are but a tide,
Ha, ha, the wooing o't.
Slighted love is sair to bide,
Ha, ha, the wooing o't.
Shall I like a fool, quoth he,
For a haughty hizzie die?
She may gae to – France for me!
Ha, ha, the wooing o't.

How it comes, let Doctors tell,
Ha, ha, the wooing o't,
Meg grew sick, as he grew hale,
Ha, ha, the wooing o't.
Something in her bosom wrings,
For relief a sigh she brings;
And O her een, they spak sic things!
Ha, ha, the wooing o't!

Duncan was a lad o' grace,
Ha, ha, the wooing o't,
Maggie was a piteous case,
Ha, ha, the wooing o't.
Duncan could na be her death,
Swelling Pity smoor'd his Wrath;
Now they're crouse and canty baith,
Ha, ha, the wooing o't.

TERMS cam – came; **o't** – of it; **blythe** – merry; **fu'** – drunk; **coost** – tossed; **fu'** – very; **asklent and unco skeigh** – askance and very disdainful; **gart** – made; **abeigh** – away from her; **fleech'd** – coaxed, flattered; **baith** – both; **grat his een baith bleer't an' blin'** – cried his eyes both bleary and blind; **spak o' lowpin o'er a linn** – spoke of jumping over a waterfall; **sair to bide** – hard to tolerate; **hizzie** – hussy; **gae** – go; **hale** – healthy; **een** – eyes; **sic** – such; **na** – not; **smoor'd** – smothered; **crouse and canty** – merry and cheerful

Green Grow the Rashes

There's nought but care on ev'ry han',
In ev'ry hour that passes, O:
What signifies the life o' man,
An' 'twere na for the lasses, O.

Chorus
Green grow the rashes, O;
Green grow the rashes, O;
The sweetest hours that e'er I spend,
Are spent amang the lasses, O.

The war'ly race may riches chase,
An' riches still may fly them, O;
An' tho' at last they catch them fast,
Their hearts can ne'er enjoy them, O.

But gie me a cannie hour at e'en,
My arms about my Dearie, O;
An' war'ly cares, an' war'ly men,
May a' gae tapsalteerie, O!

For you sae douce, ye sneer at this;
Ye're nought but senseless asses, O:
The wisest Man the warl' e'er saw,
He dearly lov'd the lasses, O.

Auld Nature swears, the lovely Dears
Her noblest work she classes, O:
Her prentice han' she try'd on man,
An' then she made the lasses, O.

TERMS **rashes** – rushes; **han'** – hand; **an' 'twere na** – if it were not;
amang – among; **war'ly** – worldly; **gie** – give; **cannie** – quiet; **e'en** –
evening; **a'** – all; **gae tapsalteerie** – go topsy-turvy; **sae douce** – so sober,
respectable; **warl'** – world; **prentice han'** – apprentice hand

I'll Ay Ca' in by Yon Town

There's nane sall ken, there's nane sall guess,
What brings me back the gate again,
But she, my fairest faithfu' lass,
And stownlins we sall meet again.

Chorus
I'll ay ca' in by yon town,
And by yon garden green, again;
I'll ay ca' in by yon town,
And see my bonie Jean again.

She'll wander by the aiken tree,
When trystin time draws near again;

And when her lovely form I see,
O haith! she's doubly dear again.

TERMS ay – always; **ca'** – call; **yon** – that; **nane sall ken** – none shall know; **brings me back the gate** – brings me back this way; **stownlins** – secretly; **bonie** – lovely; **aiken** – oak; **trystin** – meeting of lovers; **haith** – faith

 ## Ca' the Yowes to the Knowes

Chorus
Ca' the yowes to the knowes,
Ca' them whare the heather grows,
Ca' them whare the burnie rowes,
My bonie Dearie.

Hark, the mavis' evening sang,
Sounding Clouden's woods amang;
Then a-faulding let us gang,
My bonie Dearie.

We'll gae down by Clouden side,
Thro' the hazels spreading wide
O'er the waves that sweetly glide,
To the moon sae clearly.

Yonder Clouden's silent towers,

Where, at moonshine's midnight hours,
O'er the dewy-bending flowers,
Fairies dance sae cheary.

Ghaist nor bogle shalt thou fear;
Thou'rt to Love and Heav'n sae dear,
Nocht of Ill may come thee near;
My bonie Dearie.

Fair and lovely as thou art,
Thou hast stown my very heart;
I can die – but canna part,
My bonie Dearie.

TERMS ca' – drive; **yowes** – ewes; **knowes** – hillsides; **the burnie rowes** – the stream flows; **bonie** – lovely; **mavis** – song thrush; **sang** – song; **amang** – among; **a-faulding** – penning sheep; **gang, gae** – go; **sae** – so; **ghaist nor bogle** – neither ghost nor apparition; **nocht** – nothing; **stown** – stolen; **canna** – cannot

Willie Wastle

Willie Wastle dwalls on Tweed,
The spot they ca' it Linkumdoddie;
A creeshie wabster till his trade,
Can steal a clue wi' ony bodie:
He has a wife that's dour and din,
Tinkler Madgie was her mither;
Sic a wife as Willie's wife,
I wadna gie a button for her!

She has an e'e, she has but ane,
The cat has twa, the very colour;
Five rusty teeth, forbye a stump,
A clapper-tongue wad deave a miller:
A whiskin beard about her mou,
Her nose and chin they threaten ither;
Sic a wife as Willie's wife,
I wadna gie a button for her!

She's bow-hough'd, she's hem-shin'd,
Ae limpin leg a hand-bread shorter;
She's twisted right, she's twisted left,
To balance fair in ilka quarter:
She has a lump upon her breast,
The twin o' that upon her shouther;
Sic a wife as Willie's wife,
I wadna gie a button for her!

Auld baudrans by the ingle sits,
An' wi' her loof her face a-washin;
But Willie's wife is nae sae trig,
She dights her grunzie wi' a hushian;
Her waly nieves like midden-creels,
Her face wad fyle the Logan Water;
Sic a wife as Willie's wife,
I wadna gie a button for her!

TERMS dwalls – dwells; **ca'** – call; **creeshie wabster till his trade** – greasy weaver by trade; **clue** – clew (of yarn); **ony bodie** – anybody; **dour and din** – sullen and sallow; **tinkler** – tinker, gypsy; **mither** – mother; **sic** – such; **wadna gie** – would not give; **e'e** – eye; **ane** – one; **twa** – two; **forbye** – besides; **wad deave** – that would deafen; **whiskin** – whiskery; **mou** – mouth; **ither** – each other; **bow-hough'd, hem-shin'd** – bandy-legged; **ae** – one; **hand-bread** – hand's-breadth; **ilka** – every; **shouther** – shoulder; **auld baudrans** – old cat; **ingle** – fireside; **loof** – paw; **nae sae trig** – not so dainty; **dights her grunzie wi' a hushian** – wipes her snout with a rough stocking; **waly nieves** – great fists; **midden-creels** – manure baskets; **wad fyle** – would foul

My Heart's in the Highlands

Farewell to the Highlands, farewell to the
    North,
The birth-place of Valour, the country of
    Worth:
Wherever I wander, wherever I rove,
The hills of the Highlands for ever I love.

Chorus
My heart's in the Highlands, my heart is not here;
My heart's in the Highlands, a-chasing the deer;
Chasing the wild deer, and following the roe;
My heart's in the Highlands, wherever I go.

Farewell to the mountains high-cover'd with
    snow;
Farewell to the Straths and green vallies
    below;
Farewell to the forests and wild-hanging
    woods;
Farewell to the torrents and loud-pouring
    floods.

TERMS straths – broad valleys

There was a Lad

There was a lad was born in Kyle,
But whatna day o' whatna style,
I doubt it's hardly worth the while
To be sae nice wi' Robin.

Chorus
Robin was a rovin' Boy,
Rantin', rovin', rantin', rovin',
Robin was a rovin' Boy,
Rantin', rovin' Robin!

Our monarch's hindmost year but ane
Was five-and-twenty days begun,
'Twas then a blast o' Janwar' win'
Blew hansel in on Robin.

The Gossip keekit in his loof,
Quo' scho, Wha lives will see the proof,
This waly boy will be nae coof,
I think we'll ca' him Robin.

He'll hae misfortunes great an' sma',
But ay a heart aboon them a';
He'll be a credit till us a',
We'll a' be proud o' Robin!

But sure as three times three mak nine,
I see by ilka score and line,
This chap will dearly like our kin',
So leeze me on thee, Robin.

Guid faith, quo' scho, I doubt you gar
The bonie lassies lie aspar;
But twenty fauts ye may hae waur –
So blessins on thee, Robin!

TERMS whatna day o' whatna style – on what day of what style (of calendar dating); **sae** – so; **nice** – particular; **Janwar' win'** – January wind; **hansel** – a good-luck gift; **gossip** –midwife; **keekit in his loof** – looked at his palm; **quo' scho** – said she; **wha** – who; **waly** – sturdy; **nae coof** – no fool; **ca'** – call; **hae** – have; **sma'** – small; **ay** – always; **aboon** – above; **till** – to; **mak** – make; **ilka** – every; **kin'** – kind; **leeze me on thee** – I am very fond of you; **guid** – good; **gar** – make; **bonie** – pretty; **aspar** – legs apart; **fauts** – faults; **waur** – worse

John Barleycorn: A Ballad

There was three kings into the east,
Three kings both great and high,
And they hae sworn a solemn oath
John Barleycorn should die.

They took a plough and plough'd him down,
Put clods upon his head,
And they hae sworn a solemn oath
John Barleycorn was dead.

But the cheerful Spring came kindly on,
And show'rs began to fall;
John Barleycorn got up again,
And sore surpris'd them all.

The sultry suns of Summer came,
And he grew thick and strong;
His head weel arm'd wi' pointed spears,
That no one should him wrong.

The sober Autumn enter'd mild,
When he grew wan and pale;
His bending joints and drooping head
Show'd he began to fail.

His colour sicken'd more and more,

He faded into age;
And then his enemies began
To show their deadly rage.

They've taen a weapon, long and sharp,
And cut him by the knee;
Then ty'd him fast upon a cart,
Like a rogue for forgerie.

They laid him down upon his back,
And cudgell'd him full sore;
They hung him up before the storm,
And turned him o'er and o'er.

They filled up a darksome pit
With water to the brim;
They heaved in John Barleycorn,
There let him sink or swim.

They laid him out upon the floor,
To work him farther woe,
And still, as signs of life appear'd,
They toss'd him to and fro.

They wasted, o'er a scorching flame,
The marrow of his bones;
But a Miller us'd him worst of all,
For he crush'd him between two stones.

And they hae taen his very heart's blood,
And drank it round and round;
And still the more and more they drank,
Their joy did more abound.

John Barleycorn was a hero bold,
Of noble enterprise,
For if you do but taste his blood,
'Twill make your courage rise.

'Twill make a man forget his woe,
'Twill heighten all his joy;
'Twill make the widow's heart to sing,
Tho' the tear were in her eye.

Then let us toast John Barleycorn,
Each man a glass in hand;
And may his great posterity
Ne'er fail in old Scotland!

TERMS hae – have; **weel** – well; **taen** – taken

Willie Brew'd a Peck o' Maut

O Willie brew'd a peck o' maut,
And Rob and Allan cam to see;
Three blyther hearts, that lee-lang night,
Ye wad na found in Christendie.

Chorus
We are na fou, we're nae that fou,
But just a drappie in our e'e;
The cock may craw, the day may daw
And ay we'll taste the barley bree.

Here are we met, three merry boys,
Three merry boys I trow are we;
And mony a night we've merry been,
And mony mae we hope to be!

It is the moon, I ken her horn,
That's blinkin in the lift sae hie;
She shines sae bright to wyle us hame,
But, by my sooth, she'll wait a wee!

Wha first shall rise to gang awa,
A cuckold, coward loun is he!
Wha first beside his chair shall fa',
He is the King amang us three.

TERMS maut – malt; **cam** – came; **blyther** – more cheerful; **lee-lang** – livelong; **wad na found** – would not have found; **Christendie** – Christendom; **fou** – drunk; **nae** – not; **drappie** –drop; **e'e** – eye; **craw** – crow; **daw** – dawn; **ay** – always; **bree** – brew; **trow** – vow; **mony** – many; **mae** – more; **ken** – know; **blinkin** – shining; **lift sae hie** – sky so high; **wyle** – lure; **hame** – home; **a wee** – a while; **wha** – who; **gang awa** – go away; **loun** – scoundrel; **fa'** – fall; **amang** – among

The Deil's Awa wi' the Exciseman

The Deil cam fiddlin' thro' the town,
And danc'd awa wi' th' Exciseman;
And ilka wife cries, Auld Mahoun,
I wish you luck o' the prize, man.

Chorus
The deil's awa, the deil's awa,
The deil's awa wi' the Exciseman,
He's danc'd awa, he's danc'd awa,
He's danc'd awa wi' the Exciseman.

We'll mak our maut, and we'll brew our drink,
We'll laugh, sing, and rejoice, man;
And mony braw thanks to the meikle black
deil,
That danc'd awa wi' th' Exciseman.

There's threesome reels, there's foursome
reels,
There's hornpipes and strathspeys, man,
But the ae best dance e'er cam to the land
Was, the deil's awa wi' the Exciseman.

TERMS deil – devil; **awa** – away; **cam** – came; **ilka** – every; **auld Mahoun** – the Devil; **mak our maut** – make our malt; **mony braw thanks** – many fine thanks; **meikle** – great; **ae** – one; **e'er** – ever

A Man's a Man for a' That

Is there, for honest Poverty
That hings his head, an' a' that?
The coward-slave, we pass him by,
We dare be poor for a' that!
For a' that, an' a' that,
Our toils obscure, an' a' that,
The rank is but the guinea's stamp,
The Man's the gowd for a' that.

What though on hamely fare we dine,
Wear hoddin grey, an' a that?
Gie fools their silks, and knaves their wine,
A Man's a Man for a' that.
For a' that, and a' that,
Their tinsel show, an' a' that;
The honest man, tho' e'er sae poor,
Is king o' men for a' that.

Ye see yon birkie ca'd a lord,
Wha struts, an' stares, an' a' that?
Tho' hundreds worship at his word,
He's but a coof for a' that.
For a' that, an' a' that,
His ribband, star, an' a' that,
The man o' independent mind,
He looks an' laughs at a' that.

A Prince can mak a belted knight,
A marquis, duke, an' a' that;
But an honest man's aboon his might,
Guid faith, he mauna fa' that!
For a' that, an' a' that,
Their dignities, an' a' that,
The pith o' Sense, an' pride o' Worth
Are higher rank than a' that.

Then let us pray that come it may
As come it will for a' that,
That Sense and Worth, o'er a' the earth,
Shall bear the gree, an' a' that.
For a' that, an' a' that,
It's comin yet for a' that,
That Man to Man the warld o'er
Shall brithers be for a' that.

TERMS **a'** – all; **hings** – hangs; **gowd** – gold; **hamely** – homely;
hoddin grey – coarse greyish woollen cloth; **gie** – give; **e'er sae** – ever
so; **yon birkie** – that conceited fellow; **ca'd** – called; **wha** – who; **coof** –
fool; **mak** – make; **aboon** – above; **guid** – good; **mauna fa'** – must not
be like; **bear the gree** – win; **warld** – world; **brithers** – brothers

Auld Lang Syne

Should auld acquaintance be forgot
And never brought to mind?
Should auld acquaintance be forgot,
And auld lang syne?

Chorus
For auld lang syne, my jo,
For auld lang syne,
We'll tak a cup o' kindness yet,
For auld lang syne.

And surely ye'll be your pint stowp!
And surely I'll be mine!
And we'll tak a cup o' kindness yet,
For auld lang syne.

We twa hae run about the braes,
And pou'd the gowans fine;
But we've wander'd mony a weary fitt,
Sin auld lang syne.

We twa hae paidl'd in the burn,
Frae morning sun till dine;
But seas between us braid hae roar'd
Sin auld lang syne.

And there's a hand, my trusty fiere!
And gie's a hand o' thine!
And we'll tak a right gude-willie waught,
For auld lang syne.

TERMS auld – old; **lang syne** – long ago; **jo** – friend; **tak** – take; **be** – pay for; **stowp** – tankard; **twa** – two; **hae** – have; **braes** – hillsides; **pou'd** – pulled; **gowans** – daisies; **mony** – many; **fitt** – foot; **sin** – since; **paidl'd** – paddled; **burn** – stream; **frae** – from; **dine** – dinner; **braid** – broad; **fiere** – companion; **gie** – give; **gude-willie waught** – cordial drink

 McPherson's Farewell

Farewell, ye dungeons dark and strong,
The wretch's destinie!
McPherson's time will not be long
On yonder gallows-tree.

Chorus
Sae rantingly, sae wantonly,
Sae dauntingly gae'd he:
He play'd a spring, and danc'd it round,
Below the gallows-tree.

O, what is death but parting breath?
On many a bloody plain
I've dar'd his face, and in this place
I scorn him yet again!

Untie these bands from off my hands,
And bring me to my sword,
And there's no a man in all Scotland
But I'll brave him at a word.

I've liv'd a life of sturt and strife;
I die by treacherie:
It burns my heart I must depart,
And not avenged be.

Now farewell, light, thou sunshine bright,
And all beneath the sky!
May coward shame distain his name,
The wretch that dares not die!

TERMS **sae rantingly** – so merrily; **gae'd** – went; **spring** – tune; **no** – not; **sturt** – trouble

Robert Bruce's Address to His Troops at Bannockburn

Scots, wha hae wi' Wallace bled,
Scots, wham Bruce has aften led,
Welcome to your gory bed,
Or to victorie!

Now's the day, and now's the hour;
See the front o' battle lour;
See approach proud Edward's power,
Chains and Slaverie.

Wha will be a traitor-knave?
Wha can fill a coward's grave?
Wha sae base as be a Slave?
Let him turn, and flie.

Wha, for Scotland's king and law,
Freedom's sword will strongly draw,
Free-man stand, or Free-man fa',
Let him follow me.

By Oppression's woes and pains!
By your Sons in servile chains!
We will drain our dearest veins,
But they shall be free!

Lay the proud Usurpers low!
Tyrants fall in every foe!
Liberty's in every blow!
Let us Do – or Die!!!

TERMS wha hae – who have; **aften** – often; **sae** – so; **flie** – flee; **fa'** – fall

Lament of Mary, Queen of Scots, on the Approach of Spring

Now Nature hangs her mantle green
On every blooming tree,
And spreads her sheets o' daisies white
Out o'er the grassy lea:
Now Phoebus cheers the crystal streams,
And glads the azure skies;
But nought can glad the weary wight
That fast in durance lies.

Now laverocks wake the merry morn,
Aloft on dewy wing;
The merle, in his noontide bow'r,
Makes woodland echoes ring;
The mavis wild wi' mony a note,
Sings drowsy day to rest:
In love and freedom they rejoice,
Wi' care nor thrall opprest.

Now blooms the lily by the bank,
The primrose down the brae;
The hawthorn's budding in the glen,
And milk-white is the slae:
The meanest hind in fair Scotland
May rove their sweets amang;

But I, the Queen of a' Scotland,
Maun lie in prison strang.

I was the Queen o' bonie France,
Where happy I hae been;
Fu' lightly rase I in the morn,
As blythe lay down at e'en:
And I'm the sov'reign of Scotland,
And mony a traitor there;
Yet here I lie in foreign bands,
And never-ending care.

But as for thee, thou false woman,
My sister and my fae,
Grim Vengeance yet shall whet a sword
That thro' thy soul shall gae;
The weeping blood in woman's breast
Was never known to thee;
Nor th' balm that draps on wounds of woe
Frae woman's pitying e'e.

My son! my son! may kinder stars
Upon thy fortune shine!
And may those pleasures gild thy reign,
That ne'er wad blink on mine!
God keep thee frae thy mother's faes,
Or turn their hearts to thee:

And where thou meet'st thy mother's friend,
Remember him for me!

O! soon, to me, may Summer suns
Nae mair light up the morn!
Nae mair to me the Autumn winds
Wave o'er the yellow corn!
And, in the narrow house o' death,
Let Winter round me rave;
And the next flowers that deck the Spring,
Bloom on my peaceful grave.

TERMS wight – person; **durance** – imprisonment; **laverocks** – larks;
merle – blackbird; **mavis** – song thrush; **mony** – many; **brae** – hillside;
slae – sloe; **amang** – among; **maun** – must; **strang** – strong; **bonie** –
lovely; **hae** – have; **fu'** – completely; **rase** – rose; **blythe** – cheerful; **e'en**
– evening; **fae** – foe; **gae** – go; **draps** – drops; **frae** – from; **e'e** – eye;
wad – would; **nae mair** – no more

The Braes o' Killiecrankie

Whare hae ye been sae braw, lad?
Whare hae ye been sae brankie, O?
Whare hae ye been sae braw, lad?
Cam ye by Killiecrankie, O?

Chorus
An ye had been whare I hae been,
Ye wad na been sae cantie, O;
An ye had seen what I hae seen,
On the braes o' Killiecrankie, O.

I faught at land, I faught at sea,
At hame I faught my Auntie, O;
But I met the Devil and Dundee
On the braes o' Killiecrankie, O.

The bauld Pitcur fell in a furr,
An' Clavers gat a clankie, O;
Or I had fed an Athole gled
On the braes o' Killiecrankie, O.

TERMS braes – slopes; **hae** – have; **sae braw** – so fine; **brankie** –
dressed up in finery; **cam** – came; **an** – if; **wad na been** – would not have
been; **cantie** – merry; **faught** – fought; **hame** – home; **bauld** – bold; **furr** –
furrow; **gat a clankie** – got a knock; **or I had fed** – otherwise I would have
fed; **gled** – hawk

Such a Parcel of Rogues in a Nation

Fareweel to a' our Scottish fame,
Fareweel our ancient glory;
Fareweel ev'n to the Scottish name,
Sae fam'd in martial story!
Now Sark rins over the Solway sands,
An' Tweed rins to the ocean,
To mark whare England's province stands –
Such a parcel of rogues in a nation!

What force or guile could not subdue
Thro' many warlike ages,
Is wrought now by a coward few
For hireling traitors' wages.
The English steel we could disdain,
Secure in valour's station;
But English gold has been our bane –
Such a parcel of rogues in a nation!

O would, or I had seen the day
That Treason thus could sell us,
My auld grey head had lien in clay,
Wi' Bruce and loyal Wallace!
But pith and power, till my last hour,
I'll mak this declaration:
We're bought and sold for English gold –
Such a parcel of rogues in a nation!

TERMS a' – all; **sae** – so; **rins** – runs; **or** – before; **auld** – old; **lien** – lain; **mak** – make

 ## Charlie, He's My Darling

'Twas on a Monday morning,
Right early in the year,
That Charlie came to our town,
The young Chevalier.

Chorus
An' Charlie, he's my darling,
My darling, my darling,
Charlie, he's my darling,
The young Chevalier.

As he was walking up the street,
The city for to view,
O there he spied a bonie lass
The window looking thro'.

Sae light's he jimped up the stair,
And tirl'd at the pin;
And wha sae ready as hersel
To let the laddie in.

He set his Jenny on his knee,
All in his Highland dress;
For brawlie weel he kend the way
To please a bonie lass.

It's up yon heathery mountain,
An' down yon scroggy glen,
We daur na gang a-milking,
For Charlie and his men.

TERMS bonie – lovely; **sae** – so; **jimped** – jumped; **tirl'd at the pin**
– rattled the door-knocker; **wha** – who; **hersel** – herself; **brawlie weel** –
very well; **kend** – knew; **yon** – that; **scroggy** – shrubby; **daur na gang**
– dare not go

Paraphrase of the First Psalm

The man, in life wherever plac'd,
Hath happiness in store,
Who walks not in the wicked's way,
Nor learns their guilty lore!

Nor from the seat of scornful Pride
Casts forth his eyes abroad,
But with humility and awe
Still walks before his God.

That man shall flourish like the trees
Which by the streamlets grow;
The fruitful top is spread on high,
And firm the root below.

But he whose blossom buds in guilt
Shall to the ground be cast,
And, like the rootless stubble, tost
Before the sweeping blast.

For why? that God the good adore
Hath giv'n them peace and rest,
But hath decreed that wicked men
Shall ne'er be truly blest.

The First Six Verses of the Ninetieth Psalm

O Thou, the first, the greatest friend
Of all the human race!
Whose strong right hand has ever been
Their stay and dwelling-place!

Before the mountains heav'd their heads
Beneath Thy forming hand,
Before this ponderous globe itself
Arose at Thy command:

That Pow'r which rais'd and still upholds
This universal frame,
From countless, unbeginning time
Was ever still the same.

Those mighty periods of years,
Which seem to us so vast,
Appear no more before Thy sight
Than yesterday that's past.

Thou giv'st the word; Thy creature, man,
Is to existence brought;
Again Thou say'st, 'Ye sons of men,
Return ye into nought!'

Thou layest them with all their cares
In everlasting sleep;
As with a flood Thou tak'st them off
With overwhelming sweep.

They flourish like the morning flow'r,
In beauty's pride array'd;
But long ere night, cut down, it lies
All wither'd and decay'd.

Prayer, in the Prospect of Death

O Thou unknown, Almighty Cause
Of all my hope and fear,
In whose dread Presence, ere an hour,
Perhaps I must appear!

If I have wander'd in those paths
Of life I ought to shun;
As Something, loudly, in my breast,
Remonstrates I have done;

Thou know'st that Thou hast formed me
With Passions wild and strong;
And list'ning to their witching voice
Has often led me wrong.
Where human weakness has come short,
Or frailty stept aside,
Do Thou, All-Good, for such Thou art,
In shades of darkness hide.

Where with intention I have err'd,
No other plea I have,
But, Thou art good; and Goodness still
Delighteth to forgive.

Prayer, under the Pressure of Violent Anguish

O Thou Great Being! what Thou art,
Surpasses me to know:
Yet sure I am, that known to Thee
Are all Thy works below.

Thy creature here before Thee stands,
All wretched and distrest;
Yet sure those ills that wring my soul
Obey Thy high behest.

Sure Thou, Almighty, canst not act
From cruelty or wrath!
O, free my weary eyes from tears,
Or close them fast in death!

But if I must afflicted be,
To suit some wise design;
Then, man my soul with firm resolves,
To bear and not repine!